THE

Jewish Customs, Holidays, and Historical Events That Reveal Biblical Truth

EVERLASTING TRADITION

THE

Jewish Customs, Holidays, and Historical Events That Reveal Biblical Truth

EVERLASTING TRADITION

Galen Peterson

kregel
PUBLICATIONS

Grand Rapids, MI 49501

Library of Congress Cataloging-in-Publication Data
Peterson, Galen.
 The everlasting tradition: Jewish customs, holidays and historical events that reveal biblical truth / Galen Peterson.
  p. cm.
 Includes bibliographical references.
 1. Judaism—Customs and practices. 2. Bible. O.T.—Evidences, authority, etc. I. Title.
BM700.P43   1995   295.4—dc20   95-13364
                      CIP

ISBN 0-8254-3499-8 (paperback)

1 2 3 4 5 Printing / Year 99 98 97 96 95

To Sondra, who showed my
family the way to the kingdom.

And to Dawn, who walks every path with me.

CONTENTS

Part Four: Celebration

PREFACE

We live in an age where there are few secrets. Through science we are discovering the secrets of the atom and the stars. Through tabloids we are discovering the secrets of celebrities. We may even attend churches and synagogues to worship the Creator of atoms and "stars" alike. But do we truly understand that God has a very detailed plan for our lives? And do we realize that He has presented it in a most mysterious and creative manner?

This book unwraps many of those mysteries. It draws upon the specific features of both everyday and holiday customs of the Bible. It zeroes in on those elements which have either been misunderstood or have great underlying meaning. It also brings in some intriguing but little-known historical events which have profoundly shaped our perception of the message of the Bible.

There is a Hebrew folk expression that says more or less, "The apple does not fall far from the tree." This saying conveys the idea that we tend to stay close to our comfort zone, whatever it may be. But when it comes to the Bible, how many of us truly understand the cultural practices and traditions that formed the context of what we believe? These are the roots of our tree of faith. It can be said that, in many ways, our "apples" have rolled a long way down the hill from the tree which bore our fruit. We have lost track of our biblical heritage.

In the pages which follow, we will take a journey back to the place where it all began, a back-to-basics approach that will consider four primary biblical themes—tradition, blessing, redemption, and celebration. Each one will take us to a special place where we can discover what God has to say to you and to me.

We will discover that it really is no secret. There is an essential message in the Bible that permeates every chapter. But will have to look carefully in order to solve the mysteries that lie just beneath the surface. Our journey begins with a walk along the path of tradition.

PART ONE

TRADITION

CHAPTER ONE

SO WHAT'S A GOOD TRADITION?

Never tear down a fence until you find out why it was
built.   —*Will Rogers*

"Tradition! Tradition!" Now there is a word that will long
be linked to a song popularized by Tevye, the lovable character from *Fiddler on the Roof*. You can almost hear the music
whenever you come across the word.

We all can think of traditions that hold meaning for our
own lives. Without them, we lose an important link to our
past and an understanding of who we are today. There is
much that we can learn about traditions because many of
them are exceptionally valuable.

We all can think of traditions that hold meaning for our
own lives. Without them, we lose an important link to our
past and an understanding of who we are today. There is
much that we can learn about traditions because many of
them are exceptionally valuable.

Most things of real value have come about through the
trials and experiences of those who came before us. While
none of us has the personal experience of the struggles of
Revolutionary era America, we all can benefit from reading

13

their insights regarding their quest for freedom. Likewise, there is much to be learned from reading about the accounts of the lives of biblical people, from prophets and kings to farmers and fishermen.

Yet many people make the mistake of rejecting a custom or a belief simply because "it's old-fashioned." Indeed, the great American tradition, according to Ralph Waldo Emerson, was to "trample on tradition."

Today, change for the sake of variety is commonplace. Brand name, institutional, and denominational loyalty are not what they once were. Like bees in search of pollen, some people buzz from relationship to relationship, and from one spiritual stimulation to another—there to stay for awhile, yet always ready to move on to another enticing blossom. Unfortunately, as our options become ever greater, it is easy to forget the path that brought us there. In other words, many of us have lost the stability of holding on to meaningful traditions.[1]

The exact opposite can also happen in our lives. Doing something simply because "that's the way we've always done it" can be equally wrong. In this case the problem results from traditions losing their original meaning. Consider for example some of the customs based on superstition—like crossing one's fingers for good luck or knocking on wood for protection from evil. Both customs derive from the belief that power can be obtained from identifying with the cross of the Crucifixion. In the former case, the pattern of the cross is created. In the latter, the material of the cross is the object.

Another illustration of this type of action can be found in a story about a newlywed couple. One evening, the husband noticed that when his wife began to prepare a roast beef for dinner she cut off both ends of the meat before placing it in the roasting pan. He asked her why she did that. "I don't know," she said. "That's the way my mother always did it." The next time they went to the home of the wife's parents, he told his mother-in-law about the roast beef and asked her why she cut off the ends of the meat. "Well, that's the way *my* mother always did it" was her reply.

He decided that he had to get to the bottom of this mystery. So when he went with his wife to visit her grandparents, he talked to his grandmother-in-law. He said, "Your daughter and granddaughter both cut off the ends of the meat when they fix roast beef and they say, 'That's the way my mother always did it.' How about you? Why do you cut the meat in this way?" Without hesitation the grandmother replied, "Oh, that's because my roaster was too small and the only way I could get the meat to fit in it was to cut off the ends."

Sometimes that is how we follow traditions. Frequently we do something simply because somebody did it before us. Blindly *following* a tradition is, in a sense, the same as arbitrarily *forsaking* one. In both cases the underlying meaning has not been adequately explored and understood. Ask yourself, am I wise to do something without knowing what it really means? When we act without understanding, our traditions become routines and ruts. And as one sage has observed, "Beware of a rut, because it's nothing more than a grave with both ends knocked out."

Identifying a valid tradition can present a real challenge because the best traditions are not always the most popular. This principle is well-illustrated in the following episode.

In the days of the split kingdoms of Israel and Judah, a king by the name of Ahab ruled in Israel. Although the nation prospered materially during his reign, Ahab introduced the worship of a false god named Baal to the people. They overwhelmingly turned away from the one true and living God who had redeemed the nation from Egypt, and they became worshipers of Baal.

The Lord then made this pronouncement: "Yet I have left seven thousand in Israel, all the knees which have not bowed to Baal and every mouth that has not kissed him."[2] Seven thousand people remained faithful to God. Now seven thousand sounds like a lot of people. However, when we consider that there were well over a million people living in Israel at that time, in reality the faithful ones were very much in the minority.[3] The Bible calls them the "remnant." They were vastly outnumbered by those who observed the popular belief in the false god Baal.

This pattern of misguided belief was not just prevalent during the era of Elijah. Down through the centuries the truly faithful of Israel were in the minority. Moses and the Prophets alike were readily rejected while false gods and false messiahs were accepted.

Is it possible that the same situation exists today? Do people reject the truth and believe in a lie? To answer no would be a denial of human nature. History has proven that we human beings tend to get lost on the highway of life. We easily get led astray. The endless parade of enchanting leaders who have led their followers to death cannot be overlooked. But the number of followers is not the issue. It is the capability of people to believe in falsehoods that is critical. Thus, popularity cannot be the sole criterion for evaluating a tradition. There must be another way.

Fortunately, the best traditions will withstand the test of time. Somewhere in the midst of the confusion of this world are traditions with solid foundations which are as valid today as the day they were established. Our aim should be to discover them for ourselves.

This book will focus on one such tradition—the Messianic profession of faith—a tradition firmly rooted in the Hebrew Scriptures and the unique culture of ancient Israel. Yet it is still able to impact the lives of any society in any generation.

Concerning this Messianic tradition, a learned rabbi by the name of Gamaliel once said, "If it is of God, you will not be able to overthrow them; or else you may even be found fighting against God."[4] How discerning he was. He was speaking about the followers of a man named Yeshua (Jesus)* who had appeared to Israel as the Messiah in fulfillment of prophecy.

Now, many centuries later, it is commonly stated, "Jewish people do not believe in Jesus." Is this statement accurate? As a blanket statement, according to the chronicle of history, the answer is a resounding no.

Even though the majority of the people of Yeshua's day rejected him, a faithful Jewish remnant believed in him. This number of Jewish believers is far greater than what many people assume—over two hundred thousand Jews became followers of Yeshua in the first century alone. As shown by the early historian Eusebius, a very large believing community of Jewish people existed in Jerusalem until the Bar-Kochba Revolt of 132 C.E.[5,6] Recent archeological findings have confirmed that villages of Messianic Jews in the Galilee and Golan Height regions were widespread. "At two of the sites," attests Dr. Claudine Dauphin, whose work covered

---

* In keeping with the objective of presenting Jesus in His original cultural context, His actual Hebrew name, Yeshua, will be used throughout this book.

three decades of digging, "we started finding bizarre stuff—Christian symbols intertwined with Jewish symbols. It was clear that something funny was going on."[7]

This discovery is not just funny—it's exciting! Two hundred thousand people were living their lives by retaining the valued customs of their Jewish culture and by celebrating their fulfillment in the Messiah. It is a number that cannot be merely dismissed as a fringe group. Like those in Elijah's day several centuries before, they remained faithful to God's plan for their lives.

In the centuries that followed, and to our present day, a great number of Jewish people have made a belief in Yeshua their "tradition." Today, Messianic believers are still in the minority, still a remnant, but nevertheless a legitimate tradition. Remember, popularity is not the issue. The key question is this: Is it true? Is Yeshua the Messiah?

Now on the other hand, people from a non-Jewish background might wonder why it should be so important to explore a culture and customs that are not their own. Once again the same words ring true—Is Yeshua the Messiah? If this is indeed true, His message and His actions will be best understood in the context of His world. If Yeshua is not the Messiah of Israel, He cannot be the Christ of the Church.

The modern Church has suffered a great loss. After nearly two thousand years, the Church has forsaken much of its Jewish heritage. At times, the transformation has been abrupt. For example, in the fourth century the church of Constantinople mandated acceptance of this profession:

> I renounce all customs, rites, legalisms, unleavened breads and feasts of lambs of the Hebrews, sacrifices, prayers, aspersions, purifications, sanctifications and propitiations, and fasts, and new moons, and Sabbaths, and superstitions, and hymns and chants and observances and synagogues, and the food and drink of the Hebrews; in one word, I renounce absolutely everything Jewish, every law, rite and custom . . .[8]

The edge was sharp in that day. But down through the centuries there has been a steady exclusion of the Jewish roots of Christianity. To its great impoverishment, the Church has lost track of the many customs and events of Jewish history which are intimately linked with the message of the

Bible. Unfortunately, many Christians have no idea what they are missing.

Jewish or Gentile, Christian or seeker—the implications are great no matter what your background may be. Granted, reclaiming a lost tradition takes courage. In the writings of the ancient rabbis, they demonstrate how it is never too late to learn something new:

> Abraham's circumcision was postponed till he was ninety-nine years old in order that no later candidate for conversion should regard himself as too old to submit to the rite "in order not to close the door to converts."[9]

Long ago, beginning in the Garden of Eden, God made it clear that He desires to have a close and lasting relationship with humanity. His plan for securing that relationship throughout eternity is carefully interwoven in the Scriptures. It is a plan of hope which is grounded in bedrock, not shifting sand.

In the chapters which follow, we will explore that plan. As God has promised us, "you will seek Me and find Me, when you search for Me with all your heart."[10] When we endeavor to explore the Scriptures with an open heart and an open mind, we will discover a "new" tradition that is as "old" as history itself.

Chapter Two

A Little Box and a Cord of Blue

"That would be nice." Charlie Brown, after hearing that in life you win some and you lose some.
—*Charles Schulz*

Have you heard any good news lately? It often seems like we are surrounded by bad news. But sometimes bad news is only a matter of perception.

Levi Eshkol, the Prime Minister of Israel for most of the 1960's, once came to America and visited President Lyndon Johnson at the LBJ ranch in Texas. As you may know, this was a vast ranch. And Johnson loved to impress this fact upon his visitors. So he boasted to Eshkol in his Texas drawl, "Mister Prime Minister, if you get in this car and begin driving today, you will have to drive until sundown tomorrow to get across this ranch." Levi Eshkol thought to himself a moment and then replied in his best tone of humility, "Mister President, in Israel we have cars like this too."

Yes, at times, the news we hear is just a matter of perception. But there is also no getting around it, life is frequently filled with real pitfalls. Countries and marriages fail, heroes and villains die, economies and countrysides face disasters.

You can always count on the news media to keep you well-informed.

Yet in the midst of this constant bombardment of negatives, we encounter a message that is positive. It is a message that is so good that you won't hear it on the news or read about it in the newspaper. We find it in a biblical passage that stands out like a headline. It is a passage that has come to be known as the *Shema,* from the first Hebrew word of the verse, "Hear O Israel, the Lord our God, the Lord is One."

The *Shema* consists of three portions: Deuteronomy 6:4–9; 11:13–21; and Numbers 15:37–41. Among the Orthodox community, it is recited twice a day, based on the phrase, "when you lie down and when you rise up." It has been the subject of many rabbinical debates: How long after sunrise or sunset should it be said? What is the proper posture? Are women and children exempt?

Without question, the *Shema* is the central declaration of faith in every branch of Judaism. Not surprisingly, it has been the last utterance of Jewish martyrs down through the ages.

The *Shema* declares some simple, yet important principles for spiritual living. It tells us who God is, what our response to that understanding should be, and about some practical reminders for those principles. It was given because of one of our major weaknesses: it is human nature to forget.

Who Is God?

Shema Yisrael—"Hear, O Israel" (Deut. 6:4). In order to know the identity of God, we must be able to hear Him. God is to be heard. But most often, His voice is a quiet beckoning, and if we permit ourselves to be surrounded by too much "noise" we will never hear Him. In other words, if we are too busy in our lives, we will never hear God. We must stop and listen for Him.

Adonai Eloheynu—"The Lord our God." The first thing we learn about His identity is His name. The Hebrew word used in the actual Scripture of this passage is God's divine name. The transliterated Hebrew consonants are YHWH, which led some scholars to mistakenly pronounce "Jehovah." This title, also called the Tetragrammaton, means "I Am."

In the Jewish culture it has long been the custom not to

pronounce this very special name for God. The rabbinical practice has been to substitute the word *Adonai* for God's divine name whenever vocalizing biblical text. This is done out of reverence for His name and because no one is certain of its original Hebrew pronunciation. So when we hear the word *Adonai* in this verse, we know that it actually stands for another name so valued that it should not be spoken.

One thing we do know, however, "I Am" is an appellation of supreme power and character. With an image of all things springing forth from His existence, it conveys His absolute unchallenged sovereignty. He is eternal—outside the boundaries of time and space. That also means He is outside our ability to comprehend Him totally. There is a vast depth of meaning in the simplicity of the words—He is.

Adonai Echad—"The Lord is One." There are two additional characteristics that we learn about God's identity. One is that He is the only God that exists. It is a mandate for monotheism. The Bible is unequivocal in declaring Him as the sole deity of the universe. All other so-called gods are false, created by man, and unable to provide spiritual redemption.

A second characteristic is God's unique nature. *Echad* is a word that conveys composite unity, meaning more than one part in the whole. For example, in Genesis 2:24, a husband and wife are said to become *basar echad,* "one flesh." In Numbers 13:23 the spies carry *eshkol anabim echad,* "one cluster of grapes." In each case, there are multiple elements united in one entity. This is the way God chose to identify Himself. He could have used another word, *yachid,* to describe His oneness. This would have conveyed absolute unity as in the case of Genesis 22:2 where Abraham is commanded to "take your only one son."

We have the same kind of words in English. A teacher, for instance, could call upon a specific student and say, "Would *you* please read the sentence?" Or the teacher could say to the entire class, "Would *you* please read the sentence?" In the former case, "you" refers to one absolute individual, while in the latter case, "you" refers to several persons in composition. The specific type of word used greatly affects the overall meaning.

We see this crucial distinction in the *Shema,* the cornerstone of Judaism. It is a powerful testimony that within the unity of God exists more than one person. He is still one Sovereign, Almighty, Holy God, but manifested in this unique way. Christians do not believe in three Gods as some people have asserted. We fully affirm that there is no God but the Lord identified here in the *Shema*.

Many people have attempted to put God in a nice box where He can be explained and tamed. Since we are finite human beings and He is infinite in every way, it is absurd to presume that we could ever fully understand the mystery of God's nature. But clues like this one in the Shema are interspersed throughout Scripture and together they form a mosaic of remarkable assurance.

For example, one primary Hebrew word for God, *Elohim,* is in the plural form. He also uses plural pronouns when referring to Himself—"Let *us* make man in *our* image," God said.[1] Jacob wrestles with a man and then observes, "I saw God face to face."[2] In one breath, Isaiah refers to God as *Abba* (Father), *Ruach HaKodesh* (Holy Spirit) and *Moshiach* (Messiah).[3] There is definitely something highly unusual going on here!

So strong were the implications of the use of *echad* that Maimonides, the renowned rabbi of the twelfth century, substituted *yachid* in the portion on the *Shema* in his "Thirteen Articles of Faith." He wanted nothing to do with the theology of the Trinity. His conviction led him to violate the time honored tradition of preserving Scripture in its absolute purity.

Nevertheless, in the original Scriptures we see an important clue to who God is—and He is not the One many rabbis would have us believe Him to be.

Our Response

Once we know who God is, we cannot help but respond in a variety of ways:

We respond by loving
"Love the Lord your God with all your heart and with all your soul and with all your might" (Deut. 6:5). In the culture of Israel the heart was thought to be the place of your consciousness. The other two words—soul and might—were used as an added emphasis, meaning, "all of you."

The greatest act of love occurs when someone gives every-thing for you. This is a sacrificial kind of love. As Yeshua declared, "Greater love has no one than this, that he lay down his life for his friends."[4] These words are the ultimate expression of the *Shema*. They were affirmed again and again throughout the Scriptures, leaving us with a clear portrait of His plan for mankind—He would sacrifice for us.

On one occasion while discussing the *Shema* with another rabbi, Yeshua told a story which has come to be known as the Parable of the Good Samaritan. It is a tale about a Jewish man on the road between Jerusalem and Jericho who had been attacked by robbers and left to die beside the road. People who you would expect to come to his aid, religious people from his own community, passed him by. Eventually a Samaritan, a person from a nation at odds with their Jewish cousins, came along and took care of his wounds and took him to an inn where he paid for his recuperation.[5]

The Samaritan man loved him sacrificially. And he loved him unconditionally. That is the way that God loves us. It is also the way that we should treat one another.

We respond by receiving

God instructed the people of Israel in Deuteronomy 6:6 that His words must be placed "on their hearts." Since in biblical days your heart represented your consciousness and governed your actions, something must happen within you.

In a companion passage, the promise of the New Covenant in Jeremiah 31, God describes writing His Law on our hearts in the midst of the process of forgiving our sins. Only when we ask God to forgive our transgressions will our hearts be capable of receiving His way of spiritual life.

In the next two chapters we will take a closer look at our inward responses of loving God and receiving His instruc-tions on our hearts. But there is another response to God that is mandated in the *Shema*. This one is an outward response.

We respond by teaching

"And you shall teach them diligently to your sons" (Deut. 6:7). As shown here, teachers are to respond in a special manner. The word for teaching in this verse is *shahnan*. It literally means "sharpen, point, or penetrate." It doesn't mean "hammer." This is the type of teaching that "goes in easily."

And it happens that way because it occurs in the everyday affairs of life—in one's home, walking along the road, in the morning, and in the evening (v. 7). When we teach about God, we need to do it naturally and regularly.

There is a lesson here for learners, as well. The psalmist called out to God with the request, "Teach me your way, O LORD."[6] A proverb on learning which was borne from experience asserts, "Instruct a wise man and he will be wiser still; teach a righteous man and he will add to his learning."[7]

These words beg the question, "Are you teachable?" Learning is continual. Learning is lifelong. We all are students in a school that has no graduation. But it is also a place with many rewards, for God's disciples alone know who He is and are capable of loving Him, receiving His instructions, and teaching others.

Practical Reminders

What we have considered so far are basic principles for living a mature spiritual life. But in spite of the clarity of the mandate, it is simply our human nature to forget them. Have you ever forgotten someone's name just minutes or even seconds after being introduced? Occasionally I will walk into a room and suddenly realize that I have forgotten why I have gone there.

It doesn't matter how important a principle might be, these things will fade from our consciousness unless something renews their existence. God, who knows very well how we work, provided such a way for the people of Moses' day to remember His principles. He has moreover provided us with the means to remember them in our own day. They take the form of three practical reminders within the *Shema*.

Tefilin
The people of Israel were told to bind *tefilin,* meaning frontals or phylacteries to their hands and heads (Deut. 6:8). These small leather boxes containing Scripture are wrapped with leather straps to the head and one arm. Traditionally they are always used in pairs and are worn during prayer, except on the Sabbath or holidays.

Tefilin comes from the Hebrew word for prayer. Thus wearing them was to be a reminder to the people that God answers prayer. He called them a "sign." Do you look for signs from God? When you pray, do you ever ask for a sign? While God may in fact answer with a direct sign, He most often answers us by providing us with wisdom and with peace for our concerns. The bottom line is this: when we pray, God hears us, answers us, and reminds us to be faithful.

Mezuzah

The people were also told to place God's Word on the doorposts of their houses (Deut. 6:9). In obedience to this command arose the Jewish custom of the *mezuzah,* a receptacle in which Scripture was rolled and inserted. They are placed on an angle on the upper portion of the entrance to a house and "dwelling rooms."[8]

A house is a place where someone lives. The symbolism of the *mezuzah* represents two kinds of "homes" that we need to remember. First, our hearts—our place of consciousness—is the place where God's Holy Spirit dwells when we believe in Him and seek His forgiveness. Our calling is to have a suitable home for the King of the Universe to reside.

Second, God has promised to prepare special places for us to dwell in when we get to heaven.[9] When we are faithful to God and receive His plan of redemption for our lives, we can count on the greatest spiritual reward—eternal life. This is portrayed in the *Shema,* where it promises rewards for obeying God's commandments but calamity for disobeying (Deut. 11:13–21).

For their faithfulness, the people were promised rain and harvests of grain, wine and oil, grass for their cattle, and plenty of food to eat. However, for unfaithfulness there would be no rain, no produce, no life. These promises are also pictures of everlasting celebration or everlasting disaster.

Tzitziot

The final practical reminder for the people were the *tzitziot,* "tassels" or "fringes" which were attached to the four corners of their garments (Num. 15:37–41). In contemporary practice, they are attached only to a prayer shawl *(talit),* but in biblical days they were part of the everyday attire of the people. The commandment calls for wearing tassels, not the shawl.

In the midst of this commandment comes a clever visual aid. Included among the many threads of the *tzitziot* was to be one cord of blue.[10] The people were to look at the tassels and remember the things of God. The blue thread stood out as a special reminder of God's plan for their lives.

Three practical reminders—these were the ways that God showed the people how to know Him and how to respond to Him. Can you make these principles work in your life? Absolutely. We can know God in a personal way, just as the nation of Israel did long ago. We can respond to Him by loving, receiving, and teaching. And we can maintain some practical reminders, too.

Some people might be able to follow the practices of *tefilin, mezuzah,* and *tzitziot,* and keep a proper focus. But for those who are not inclined to ritual observance, the same objective can still be achieved. We can maintain a regular prayer life in which God reveals His will and builds our spiritual character. We can read His Scriptures and discover His many truths. And we can be with other people who are walking the same path and, like threads of blue, will help remind us to be faithful.

Yes, our memories are short. But we are not without some effective ways to remember the deepest lessons in life. When we are faithful in applying God's plan to our lives, then it can be said about us:

Hear O my people. God has done a great thing on your behalf. Just as He preserved Israel and taught them how to keep His commandments, He has redeemed you and will reveal His wisdom and guidance for your life each and every day.

Don't ever forget it. It's the best news you will ever hear.

CHAPTER THREE

DO YOU REALLY LOVE GOD?

Love is a form of flattery which pleases all, . . . even God.
—Ludwig Boerne

It was my first trip to Israel. My wife Dawn and I enjoyed the experience of speaking to people wherever we went. One day, while walking along a sidewalk in Tel Aviv, we stopped a man who was approaching us in order to find out how far it was to a certain street. I asked him, "How many blocks is it to Dizengoff Street?" "Oh," he answered, "about four thousand blocks." Four thousand blocks? No, that could not be right. Four thousand blocks! That would stretch to Egypt.

I suppose I looked a bit perplexed as I asked him how long a block was. He responded, "About twelve inches." Twelve inches? At that point we thanked him and said goodbye. As he headed off down the street, my wife and I looked at each other and together we figured out what the man was saying. He thought blocks meant building blocks or bricks which are about one foot long, not city blocks. That meant Dizengoff Street, by his reckoning, was about four thousand feet, or four thousand blocks away. It was all a matter of miscommunication. No doubt he also thought those Americans have a strange way of measuring distances.

Communication is paramount in any society or in any age. It is the primary means we have in understanding one another. It is especially hard to communicate with someone when you are out of touch with them. That's true in interpersonal relationships and in our relationship with God. God, as we have already seen, knows our tendencies well. And so He gave us some ways to keep that relationship alive.

He instituted prayer so that we might be able to communicate our appreciation for His goodness and our heartaches for the times when things go wrong. He called us to fellowship where we can share with others our joys and our sorrows. He also created a series of special events, the biblical festivals, which provided a venue for interaction between God and mankind.

In the days of the Temple in Jerusalem, these holidays formed a schedule of activities which kept the anticipation level of the people high. By repeating the festivals year after year, the people became well-acquainted with their obligations and the symbolic implications of the associated rituals. Their continuity reinforced the spiritual maturation process of those who desired to be faithful to the Lord.

Three times a year—for the feasts of Passover, Pentecost, and Tabernacles—the people of Israel would make a pilgrimage to Jerusalem for a tremendous spiritual celebration. It was quite literally a "mountaintop experience." After each journey, a quiet time then followed as they resumed their everyday lives. But in spite of the frequency of the festivals, it was easy to get caught up in the everyday affairs of life once they had returned from the mountain. So a custom was initiated that would keep God in the midst of their lives and would help keep their love for Him from fading.

It was called the *omer*. Meaning a "sheaf," it was an offering of the first cutting of barley. On the day after the Sabbath which followed Passover, a few stalks of grain were bound together and presented in the Temple to the Lord of the harvest.

The *omer* also came to be associated with the period of time that led up to *Shavuot,* the Hebrew name for Pentecost, or the Feast of Weeks.[1] For that fifty day interval a special custom arose and is still observed today. Like marking off days on a calendar, a counting benediction is said for fifty days:

> Blessed art Thou, O Lord our God, King of the universe, who has sanctified us by Thy commandments, and has commanded us concerning the counting of the Omer.
>
> This is the ___ day, being ___ weeks and ___ days of the Omer.

The actual number of the day is inserted each day until the fiftieth day when Shavuot is celebrated. For instance, half-way through the days of counting, a person would say, "This is the twenty-fifth day, being three weeks and four days of the Omer." Traditionally, some people add the words from Psalm 67 since it has exactly seven verses and forty-nine words. Also during this period, partial mourning is observed. People do not cut their hair, concerts are not held, and weddings are not performed.[2] These restrictions have evolved since the original instructions were given in the Torah, however.

At its inception, the *omer* was intended to keep a focus on the ways of God in anticipation of the next great event on the calendar. That kind of anticipation keeps our love for God fresh and renewed day by day. This may be a good measurement of our love for God: it is not how we respond during those great mountaintop experiences, but how we respond in the daily grind of the valley.

This leads us to a fundamental question—do you love God? And if your answer is yes, how can you know if you truly love Him?

There is a cost to commitment. The person who stays faithful to God will inevitably face ridicule for his or her faith. The psalmist wrestled with this very issue. When he came to a time of personal struggle on his spiritual journey, he acknowledged:

> But as for me, my feet had almost slipped; I had nearly lost my foothold. For I envied the arrogant when I saw the prosperity of the wicked. They have no struggles; their bodies are healthy and strong. They are free from the burdens common to man; they are not plagued by human ills. All day long I have been plagued; I have been punished every morning.[3]

Mention the word Christian today and many people picture a naive old-fashioned buffoon, or worse still, a hypocrite wanting to put another notch on his belt of souls. Jewish believers face double ridicule for their faith. It takes a lot of *chutzpah* to believe in Yeshua and still live a Jewish lifestyle. Become a Buddhist, follow the New Age, believe in astrology—and you can still feel welcome in the synagogue. But following Yeshua is seen as a complete betrayal in the Jewish world.

There is, without question, a price to pay for remaining faithful to God. But is it worth it? Yes, the value received as a believer is indeed priceless. The person who truly loves God has the promise of eternal life. The person who truly loves God is also building the kind of character that can withstand any form of attack, whether it be persecution for who you are, or the daily kinds of conflicts that tend to wear down our self-esteem.

After struggling with the apparent success of nonbelievers and the seemingly endless trials of believers, the psalmist finally understood the reality behind all this. He realized that their "final destiny" would be ruin and he took comfort in knowing "the Sovereign LORD is my refuge."[4]

A genuine love for God and a strong personal character—these are noble goals for our lives. But how can we move beyond merely desiring these attributes and setting goals to actually possessing them? To obtain meaning in our lives can be a frustrating experience. Usually we resort to religious formulas to satisfy that need.

- If I go to the synagogue or to church every week . . .
- If I say certain prayers the right number of times a day . . .
- If I read through the Bible seven times a year . . .
- If I stringently observe dietary laws . . .
- . . . then I will be right with God.

Is that what God is really looking for? Here is what the prophet Micah had to say:

> With what shall I come before the LORD and bow down before the exalted God? Shall I come before him with burnt offerings, with calves a year old? Will the LORD be pleased with thousands of rams, with ten thousand rivers of oil? Shall I offer my firstborn for my transgression, the fruit of my body

for the sin of my soul? He has showed you, O man, what is good. And what does the LORD require of you? To act justly and to love mercy and to walk humbly with your God.[5]

Offerings are good, assembling for worship is good, praying and reading the Bible is good, eating kosher is good. But these are just ends to a means. There has to be something deeper on the inside. Without the invisible attributes of justice, mercy, and humility, what we do visibly matters little.

That is why so many people have rejected Yeshua down through the years. Some people were looking for an outward King who would solve the problems of living in a world tainted with corruption. Others were looking for a powerful King whom they could use for their own manipulative purposes. God, who is the Supreme Judge, will ultimately take care of the abuses of justice and power. But He is also concerned about what lies within each and every one of us on a most personal level. That is why Messiah came—to become King of our hearts before He could become King in a national sense.

God has made it clear that He is not interested in religious ritual alone. At one point, He said more or less, "I've had enough of all these animal sacrifices, incense, and holy assemblies. What I'd really like to see is some personal character, manifested by caring for others and by repentance."[6]

The person who meets that kind of description is showing sincere love toward God. Loving God is a conscious, voluntary kind of action. It is something that will never happen without making a commitment to follow through.

The *omer* is like that. One day at a time, but without missing a day, we need to affirm our relationship to God. We need to offer to Him the very best that we have, as if we are cutting stalks of grain, and presenting them to the Lord. He wants to know that we will not value material things over people. He wants to know that we will set aside time to talk with Him in prayer. And He wants to know that we will worship Him with sincerity. When we give priority to God, we are communicating our love to Him.

But it surely helps when we realize by reading His communication to us—the Bible—that He loves us, too. Here is one way of expressing a healthy attitude of love toward God:[7]

If I pray to God with words that I really don't mean, I don't really love Him. If I know every story in the Bible and can even work miracles, but do not love God, it means nothing. If I do good deeds because I am supposed to and not because I really care for another person, I do not benefit personally.

My love for God will make me patient. I need to wait for Him to answer me in His own timing. My love for God means that I will not envy the blessings that He bestows upon others, neither will I give others the impression that He favors me over anyone else. I will not readily get angry toward God if something does not go my way; I will not say to Him, "it's just not fair." My love for God will move me to sorrow for those who reject Him and to joy when someone believes in Him.

My love for God will persevere even when the circumstances of life make it difficult. When those around me fail Him, it will be no excuse for me to stop being faithful. All the things which I do to demonstrate my faith are just the beginning, and my love for God will grow deeper still, until the day He calls me home.

And now these three remain: the ways in which I express my faith, my hope that Messiah will return soon, and my love of God. But the greatest of these is my love of God.

Every day, not just during the *omer,* is another day to count the many things that God has done on our behalf. Each and every day we can count on His unfailing love for us. That is a given.

But there is one final question that remains unsettled. It doesn't have to do with *us* doing the counting, but conversely— can God count on you?

C H A P T E R   F O U R

WRITTEN ON YOUR HEART

It took six days to make the world, forty to give the Torah.
—*Amora Simhai*

Somewhere in the craggy wilderness east of the Red Sea stands a peak jutting from the desert floor. Like a massive arena in the midst of a modern city, Mount Sinai served as the site of an encounter of epic proportions during the Exodus. For it was there that God revealed the *Torah,* the Law, to His people Israel.

It is an event commemorated each year on the holiday of *Shavuot,* the Feast of Pentecost. A well-conceived rabbinical tradition holds that the Law was given to Moses precisely on this very day.[1] Thus, in contemporary practice, the Torah is a central theme on this holiday.

But is the *Torah* alone the final culmination of God's revelation? The answer lies in the account of that great transaction in the wilderness as told in Exodus 19. From this chapter, we learn God's detailed plan in seven progressive steps:

The Nation of Israel: Their Purpose

Fifty days after their release from slavery in Egypt, the nation of Israel camped at the base of Mount Sinai. A great transition was imminent—the slaves of Pharaoh were about to become servants of the Lord. Moses, the one who had led them forth, was now called up to the summit in order to hear God's instructions.

As the people were about to receive the *Torah,* they needed to know the importance of being obedient and the importance of helping one another be obedient. God called them to be "a kingdom of priests and a holy nation" (v. 6).

The Hebrew word for priest, *kohane,* describes a person who was responsible for "mediating" and "officiating." A priest is someone who does something on behalf of another person. Beginning that day on Mount Sinai, the Law would require two types of priestly actions.

First, priests were needed to conduct ceremonial responsibilities on behalf of all the people. Through specialized training this would be their lifelong vocation. These priests, who were limited to the tribe of Levi, would be charged with receiving offerings from the rest of the people and then presenting them sacrificially to the Lord.

A second group of priests came from the general population—everyone else! The people themselves would have daily responsibilities toward one another as a unit. No one was exempt from serving others in this kingdom of priests. Everyone was charged with helping his or her neighbor be obedient and faithful to the Lord. Everyone had a purpose in God's plan for the nation.

Their Promise

So having heard their commissioning, they gave in return their promise. "The people all responded together, 'We will do everything the LORD has said'" (v. 8). Talk about good intentions!

Can you relate to that kind of response? At times we all make promises that we will never keep. New Year's Day is a famous time for making resolutions for the upcoming year which can be more realistically measured in hours. Marriage vows, made to last a lifetime, can fade into memory once the honeymoon is over. We're good at making promises, but poor at keeping them.

One legend holds that God approached every nation with the prospect of receiving the Law, but none would accept it until He came to Israel. He knocked at seventy doors (the number of nations at that time), but only Israel answered and said, "We will do everything the LORD has said."[2]

This legend is fanciful speculation, yet it does recognize one profound fact: there was but one revelation of God's Law and the nation of Israel gladly received it. Now, whether or not the people knew what they were getting into, that is quite another matter!

In spite of the naiveté of the people, God knew better. Becoming a holy nation was not something to be taken lightly. He would motivate them to be serious about their promise.

Their Preparation

God knew that they needed to be spiritually prepared before they could take upon the responsibility as a kingdom of priests. They were told to take three days to consecrate themselves, meaning to "set themselves apart." They were even instructed to wash their clothes in an act of ritual purity (v. 10). It would be a sign of internal purity, a purity of character.

One example we have in our modern culture to being set apart for preparation for a goal is spring training in major league baseball. Each year, hundreds of rookies and veterans head to Florida and Arizona to begin preparing for the upcoming season. Batting practice, running the bases, and countless repetitions of the double play and hitting the cutoff man fill the days of these athletes. They toil in special facilities set apart from their far away homes, and at the end of each day, their clothes really need a good washing!

So it was for the nation of Israel. They were about to be called up to the spiritual big leagues. As a result, they were to take some steps that demonstrated the importance of the day. Each person could see everyone else making the preparations. There was a unity of action, but there was likely much time also for personal introspection.

Their Problem

The Bible underscores the reason for the three days of preparation. It was because the people had a problem. The narrative reads like a Steven Spielberg movie script:

On the morning of the third day there was thunder and lightning, with a thick cloud over the mountain, and a very loud trumpet blast. Everyone in the camp trembled. Then Moses led the people out of the camp to meet with God, and they stood at the foot of the mountain. Mount Sinai was covered with smoke, because the LORD descended on it in fire. The smoke billowed up from it like smoke from a furnace, the whole mountain trembled violently, and the sound of the trumpet grew louder and louder. Then Moses spoke and the voice of God answered him.[3]

According to ancient legend, thunder and lightning kept the children of Israel awake while Moses was on Mount Sinai waiting to receive the Law. Today in commemoration of this legend, people in Orthodox homes stay up all night reading *Torah.*

But the problem faced by the Israelites was more than just lack of sleep. Their greater problem was how to have a personal relationship with a holy God. God is holy; people are not. He is pure and truthful and righteous. We are tainted with impure thoughts and actions; we lie, cheat, and steal. It is a problem so great that a vast gulf exists between Him and us.[4] Because of God's holiness, He commanded that limits for the people be placed around the mountain and that they be informed that they would die if they went up there (v. 12).

The Law itself set "boundaries" on holiness. It revealed what sin was. A closer examination of the word *Torah* illustrates this principle. *Torah* comes from the root *yarah,* meaning to "flow" or to "lay out." The Law laid out before the people the boundaries on their conduct. It revealed that actions beyond those boundaries—what it called sin—would be unacceptable to the Most Holy God.

The New Testament sheds some additional light on the understanding of *Torah.* In the letter to the Galatians, the word *paidagogos,* "a boy leader," is used to describe the Law.[5] This was a servant whose role was to take children to school. Thus the Law, in this figure of speech, takes us to a place where we find out what our failings are—it doesn't create them. The Law was given to show us that we are all missing the mark of holiness.

Back at the foot of Mount Sinai, "everyone in the camp trembled." Do you ever feel like God is making you tremble?

If not, perhaps you need to reconsider God's holiness. Nothing will make us "tremble" more than to realize that we are sinners and one day we will stand before Him in judgment. That is truly a great problem.

Their Priest

On behalf of Israel, God provided a way out of their dilemma. We have seen how a priest was to be a mediator, one who went between persons. The nation of Israel needed a very special individual to be their grand mediator to go between a holy God and sinful humanity. It was Moses.

Moses was called to a direct face-to-face meeting with God. He beheld God's holiness; he was touched by His radiance. Moses was given the *Torah*. He then brought it to the people and they were to observe the commandments faithfully. For the time being, Moses would carry out this role of mediation. But as a man, he would have his own failings and ultimately, like everyone else, he would die.

Over the centuries, many would try to keep the Law, but without exception, the people would fail sooner or later. They needed something that would be perfect in dealing with their inability to cope with holiness on their own. They needed someone who could understand the struggles of being a human being, yet could live a life of perfection, fulfilling the Law in every aspect. There could be no greater way of mediation. They needed Messiah.

Their Perfect Fulfillment

The written *Torah* was a foreshadowing of a more perfect law, a more perfect way to come. It would be one "written on their hearts." In chapter two we saw how this was God's ideal plan for His people and that it centered around the forgiveness of our sin.

Listen to the way the prophet Ezekiel expresses God's plan: "I will give you a new heart and put a new spirit in you; I will remove from you your heart of stone and give you a heart of flesh."[6]

The *Torah* was something literally chiseled in stone. It was codified. Some scholars have said that the Law was also accompanied by an oral tradition which elaborated on the finer points. In fact, there is a humorous legend that God even handed down the recipe for chicken soup on Mount Sinai!

One thing is for certain, the Law was an extremely difficult thing to understand and to observe.

It was widely understood that when Messiah came, He would teach the purest understanding of the Law. But as foreshadowed in the writings of the prophets, he would do something that would remove the heavy burden of having to keep perfectly the Law. He would personally bear the consequences of our failures. He would pay the price for our forgiveness and redemption.

How can we know this is true? How would people of Israel and other nations come to know that they were missing the mark and that Messiah provided the way of overcoming the consequences?

Their Prophesied Paraclete

God's solution was to send the *parakletos*—The "Intercessor." In the days of the Old Testament, God's Holy Spirit was not universally and continually present with all mankind. He moved in and out of circumstances on earth.

But His enduring presence would later accompany the New Covenant brought into effect through Yeshua. Speaking on behalf of God, Ezekiel confirms this solution by saying, "I will put my Spirit in you and move you to follow my decrees and be careful to keep my laws."[7]

The unceasing presence of God's Holy Spirit would show people how to live truly spiritual lives. He would teach them the fine points. He would convict their hearts to lead them to repentance. He would reveal the truth regarding Messiah. And He would comfort them and give them peace. That is how they would be able to live with God's Law written on their hearts.

It would also result in momentous changes in this world simply because of His remaining presence. The prophet Joel unveiled God's ultimate plan to pour out His "Spirit on all people" and that "everyone who calls on the name of the LORD will be saved."[8] A day would come when God would "pour out" His Spirit, not only on the nation of Israel, but on all people.

Yes, the giving of the Law on Mount Sinai was a great event. But as we have seen, the implications go far deeper than just receiving rules and regulations for religious observance. It revealed God's complete panorama of redemption.

The giving of the Law was just the beginning of God's action plan for this world. As we stand before Him, perched on our own mountain in the wilderness, we face a very personal commissioning:

- Just as Israel was given the purpose of being a kingdom of priests—we are called to minister to one another.
- Just as they promised to do His will—we need to dedicate ourselves to faithfully follow His ways.
- Just as they prepared themselves in ritual purity—we need to cleanse our lives from sin by asking God's forgiveness.
- Just as their problem was how to have a relationship with a holy God—sin in our lives will prevent us from having a healthy, abiding relationship with God, not just on a daily basis, but throughout eternity.
- Just as they needed a higher mediator, a more capable priest to go between them and God—we too need a High Priest, Messiah, to go between us and our Heavenly Father.
- Just as the Law was promised to become perfected in their hearts—God's ways become perfected in our own hearts when we turn from our sins and seek His forgiveness.
- And just as God's Holy Spirit was promised to come upon His people in a powerful way—we receive the encouragement and the power of His unfailing presence when we become believers in Messiah.

Like the traditions of the *Shema* and the *Omer,* the giving of the *Torah* bears the imprint of the almighty God. But we are beckoned to take a step beyond tradition—to explore another biblical cornerstone—the abundant blessings of the Creator.

PART TWO

BLESSING

CHAPTER FIVE

BLESSINGS, BLESSINGS, EVERYWHERE

I have been driven to my knees many times because there was no place else to go.　*—Abraham Lincoln*

There is a Hebrew blessing for virtually everything in this world. There are blessings for following God's ordinances, for times of praise and thanksgiving, and for experiences of enjoyment.

Each of them begins with a basic affirmation of God's sovereignty, "Blessed are You, O Lord our God, King of the universe," followed by a specific acknowledgment of His accomplishments. For example, upon hearing thunder, the prescribed blessing is:

> Blessed are You, O Lord our God, King of the universe, whose might and power fill the world.

On seeing a rainbow:

> . . . who remembers the Covenant, is faithful to the Covenant and keeps His word.

On seeing beautiful trees or animals:

> . . . who has withheld nothing from this world and has
> created beautiful creatures and beautiful trees in it, so that
> people may delight in them.

Others have been developed for enjoying freedom, for new
clothes, for smelling fragrant spices, and the more widely-
known blessings over bread and wine. As it is said in the
Talmud, "Anything which is enjoyed requires a blessing."[1]

In the *Fiddler on the Roof,* Tzeitel, one of Tevye's
daughters, asks the rabbi if there is a blessing for a sewing
machine. He replies, "There is a blessing for everything"
and then procedes to pray for the sewing machine. At another
time the rabbi is asked if there is a blessing for the Tsar of
Russia and he cleverly responds, "A blessing for the Tsar?
Of course. May God bless and keep the Tsar—far away from
us!"

Even Herbert Hoover, the thirty-first president of the United
States, picked up on the blessing custom when he once
quipped, "Blessed are the young, for they shall inherit the
national debt."

Blessing is a word that is used so often that it is easy to
miss the significance of its basic meaning. One person sneezes
and another is bound to say immediately, "God bless you."[2]
Many of us say with regularity words to the effect, "That
was a real blessing." We all would do well to take a closer
look at the biblical concept of blessings—to investigate their
purposes and to become challenged to not take them for
granted.

Blessings Are for Everyone

In Psalm 115 we hear God's promise to "bless the house of
Israel" (v. 13). But in the very next verse it says, "He will
bless those who fear the LORD," a phrase used throughout the
Scriptures for non-Jews who believe in the God of Israel. God
is not an elitist when it comes to blessings. Nations, ethnic
groups, denominations, genders, or age groups—we're all eli-
gible for God's blessings.

The psalmist wraps it all up with the words, "small and
great alike." Do you ever feel like, "what difference am I to
God. I'm just a puny speck among billions of people"?

Part of the problem that we face with significance and self-esteem is that we tend to measure God's blessings with a human yardstick. Our values are not always God's values. We lose track of God's perspective. We need to be reminded that in God's eyes, He loves us all equally and unconditionally.

In order to demonstrate this kind of love, God has given us one incomparable blessing that we all can enjoy. As part of God's covenant with Abraham we encounter these intriguing words: "all peoples on earth will be blessed through you."[3] When Abraham heard these words, he probably had no idea what that blessing would be at the time. But God had something very specific in mind. Here was His plan—through Abraham was born Isaac, and to Isaac was born Jacob, and his son was Judah, and many generations later came David, and from him ultimately descended Yeshua.[4]

God's promise was the Messianic blessing. Through Messiah, all the peoples on earth can enjoy the fruits of His coming—a spiritual peace and a purpose for living plus the greatest blessing, life everlasting. Let there be no doubt—the blessing of Messiah is for everyone; it is for you.

Some Blessings are Diverse in Nature

While we share in a common Messianic hope, we do experience a variety of personal blessings in His earthly kingdom. One passage which demonstrates this kind of diversity is Deuteronomy 33. Just before Moses died, he pronounced some blessings upon the Israelites unique to their individual tribes.

Some blessings were based on the needs of tribes. Reuben at one time faced extinction—so their blessing was the promise of preservation.[5] Judah faced strong foes—their blessing would be divine protection from their foes.

One blessing was based on responsibilities. The Levites, the priestly tribe, were granted the Thummim and the Urim. These stones were used to ascertain the will of God in particular situations.

Another blessing was based on future significance. Benjamin needed security in order to safeguard the future site of Jerusalem.

Some blessings were based on material affluence. Joseph (represented in this passage by his two sons, Ephraim and Manasseh) would receive an abundance of agricultural prosperity. Zebulun and Issachar's success would come in the form of commercial enterprise.

Some blessings were based on empowerment for service. Gad was on the frontlines of conquering the Promised Land. Both Dan and Naphtali were adventurous and dwelled on the outer boundaries. They were all given special abilities to live on the frontier.

A final blessing was based on a lifetime of productivity. Asher would have productive olive groves and they would be characterized by their longevity.

In a way, these blessings are a picture of God's blessing and equipping of the household of faith. In the New Covenant we are shown how God gives believers different gifts to complete a mosaic of ministries and that each person has his or her own unique set of gifts.[6]

But there is another way to look at the implications of the blessings of the twelve tribes. We need to realize in a more general sense that everyone is not blessed in the same way:

- We all have different needs.
- We all have different responsibilities.
- None of us knows the specific future significance of our lives, except that our faith in Messiah means dwelling with Him in the hereafter.
- We all receive different material blessings.
- Not all of us are empowered for the same kind of service.
- Each of us will have different degrees of productivity and longevity.

Blessings are gifts from God. And if they are gifts, how can we be jealous when someone else has a different blessing, or a "better" blessing? That's easy to do. But if our heart is right, we can say like Moses: "There is no one like the God of Yeshurun (a poetic variant for Israel), who rides on the heavens to help you and on the clouds in his majesty."[7]

These words describe an attitude. In order to enjoy truly the select blessings that God has in store for us, whatever they may be, we must be ready to receive them.

Blessings Call for Humility

One by one they came, families from villages all around. Parents carried their youngest children while older ones walked alongside. Up the dusty paths they hiked until they came upon the site where Yeshua had paused to speak to the people.

Families gathered around and placed their children before him and there, as Mark describes in the tenth chapter of his Gospel, "he took the children in his arms, put his hands on them and blessed them."[8]

This is a custom that has long been a part of the Jewish culture. Since Talmudic times, Jewish parents have observed the custom of blessing children on the Sabbath. The father says to his sons: "May God make you like Ephraim and Manasseh." For daughters the blessing is: "May God make you like Sarah, Rebecca, Rachel, and Leah." In each case, heroes of Israel have been selected as the ideal models for blessing.[9] The parents hope that God will be gracious and compassionate unto the children just as He was to the esteemed ancestors of the nation.

This custom also fosters a special bonding with those who came before us. There is a benefit in understanding who we are when making that kind of connection to previous generations. In addition, there is an intimacy and a sense of value that grows between parents and their children in this custom. The parent who demonstrates a desire for God's blessing upon his or her children will positively impact them for the rest of their lives. This kind of commitment is a declaration of individual worth and importance that is often lacking in our world.

As the children came to Yeshua, they experienced this kind of special moment. He touched them and He blessed them. But He took it to a deeper level by using this custom as a symbol of the greatest blessing of all—"receiving the kingdom of God."[10] He signified that a place in the kingdom of God comes about when people present themselves before their heavenly Father like little children.

For us to receive God's greatest blessings, including a place in His kingdom, we need a childlike faith, a childlike curiosity, and a childlike humility. That means a faith that encourages questions but relies on the wisdom of the Lord to set the terms and the results. This kind of attitude requires flexibility and a sense of vulnerability that says, "take me just as I am."

But the story does not end at this point. In this passage we

are immediately shown a contrasting situation in which a
person's attitude precludes him from receiving a blessing.
Verse 17 tells us that "a man ran up to Him and fell on his
knees."

Barak, "to bless," has the same Hebrew root as the human
knee, *berek.* There is a definite symbolic picture in this word.
It depicts a subject on his or her knees before a king. The
king's will alone determines whether or not he will grant a
favor to a subject. The king has the power, the subject has
none. But the attitude of the subject will go a long way in
determining the king's motivation to extend his blessing. In
other words, blessings originate from someone with *authority*
and they are given to someone in *humility.*

The man who came before Yeshua understood the cultural
posture of blessing. He went right to his knees.[11] Yeshua was
prepared to grant the blessing. In fact it says He "looked at
him and loved him."[12] Yet with great discernment He knew
that the man was on his knees on the outside, but holding
back on the inside. When He called to the man to set aside
the things of this world and to follow Him, the man refused to
do so.

The man on his knees knew the protocol, the way to work
the system, but his heart was not right—he lacked a childlike
humility. That, then is where genuine blessings rest—at the
feet of the Creator. But not in a superficial fashion. It is not
enough to make a token acknowledgement here and there, in
making all the right moves so others can see us.

Take another look at the words from the various custom-
ary blessings at the beginning of this chapter. Each time, the
object of the blessing is not the bread or the wine or the
rainbow, it is God Himself. He is the One who created them
and is worthy of our praise. These blessings are not a formula
for getting things. They are an opportunity to state our proper
relationship to our Master.

We need to come into God's presence with faith, curiosity,
and humility like a child sitting in the lap of a parent. When
our hearts are right before Him, He knows what is best for
us, and He will grant to us His very select blessings.

Make a little self-diagnosis today. Are you enjoying God's
grace and unique favor in your life? Or is there some envy or
self-centered craving from which you need to be released?

Blessings rest at the feet of the Creator. When we place

ourselves before Him in absolute humility, He truly has some exciting things in store for us. In the next three chapters we will look at three episodes in the Scriptures that are told with the barest of details. But behind each reference is an untold story abounding in God's blessings.

CHAPTER SIX

MESSIAH WAS NOT BORN ON CHRISTMAS

When will Messiah come? Today if you hearken to His
voice.   *—Rabbi Simeon ben Yohai*

Chestnuts roasting on an open fire. Away in a manger.
Grandma got run over by a reindeer. Popularized in song,
these are all images of Christmas. Some people revel in the
giving (and receiving!) of gifts. Most Christians endeavor to
focus on the "real meaning of Christmas." Most Jewish people
try as best they can to stay clear of the holiday altogether.

Is it possible that we are all missing the boat to a certain
extent on this one? Where is the legitimate common ground
of historical accuracy and spiritual meaning upon which we
all can stand? Once again, the Scriptures hold the key.

The God Who Dwells Among Us

One thing is apparent in the Bible. In spite of our failings
and idiosyncrasies, God really wants our company. He repeatedly has indicated that He desires to dwell with us.

A continual thread of intimacy between God and humanity is woven into the Scriptures. At times it is strong—as in
the Garden of Eden or when the nation of Israel lived in

---

right-eousness. But at other times it is broken—as in the Fall
when Adam and Eve were expelled from the Garden or when
the nation of Israel pursued idolatry.

Nevertheless, time and time again, God took steps to knot
this frayed thread together. In the Garden, He walked alongside Adam and Eve. In the Sinai wilderness He expressed,
"Have them construct a sanctuary for me and I will dwell
among them."[1] Within that Tabernacle, and later in the
Temple in Jerusalem, resided His *shekhinah* ("radiance"), also
known as His *kavod* ("glory cloud").

Even while the Temple was standing, He unveiled His
desire for an even more intimate form of dwelling—as Messiah, He would come to live on earth. He would walk and talk
and feel emotion as we do. He would experience ridicule and
temptation (though without giving in). He would be called
Immanuel, a Hebrew title meaning "God with us." The prophet
Isaiah foretold his coming by recording:

> Therefore the LORD himself will give you a sign: The virgin
> will be with child and will give birth to a son, and will call
> him Immanuel.[2]

> For to us a child is born, to us a son is given, and the govern-
> ment will be on his shoulders. And he will be called Wonderful
> Counselor, Mighty God, Everlasting Father, Prince of Peace.[3]

These proclamations are most extraordinary. Some scholars have mistakenly disputed the virgin birth of Yeshua,[4] but
in the midst of all the controversy, it is easy to overlook the
messianic designation of *Immanuel.* He would be much more
than an indication that "God is on their side," He would
physically walk among them. In keeping with the revelation
of the tri-unity of God (as demonstrated in the *Shema* and
other passages in chapter two), Messiah would be born into
the human race as a Son, but fully retaining His divine nature. Can you think of a more profound way that God could
demonstrate His interest in our lives than to come and dwell
among us?

Another prophet, Daniel, while in Babylonian captivity,
brought to light the actual era when Messiah would come. He
prophesied that Messiah would come in sixty-nine weeks of
years—173,880 days to be exact—after the decree to restore

and rebuild Jerusalem was issued.[5] Now there is a bold statement with incredibly specific detail. Nearly a century later, two declarations were issued by King Artaxerxes I of Persia.[6] The first in 458 B.C.E. enabled a contingent of exiles to return under the leadership of Ezra in order to reestablish the law in Jerusalem. The second came in the year 445. When he made it official in the spring of that year that the walls of Jerusalem could stand once again, the Messianic countdown began. The prophetic clock would tick off the days until Messiah's coming.

We are left with the undeniable conclusion that Messiah had to come in the early part of the First Century C.E.—not at any other time in history! In fact, some scholars have calculated the precise date when this Messianic countdown reached zero.[7] What happened 173,880 days after Artaxerxes said, "rebuild Jerusalem"? A Galilean named Yeshua entered Jerusalem on a donkey just as the prophet Zechariah had said the Messiah would do. The crowds cried out, "Hosanna to the Son of David" as they laid palm branches before Him in recognition of His messianic credentials. Exactly as Daniel had predicted, on that spring day just before Passover in 33 C.E., Yeshua was first publicly heralded as Messiah.[8]

Coincidence? Hardly. We know from Deuteronomy 18:21–22 that the sign of a true prophet was one hundred percent accuracy. There could be no room for error in their predictions. Daniel was such a man. He made a bold prophecy. And his words were fulfilled perfectly nearly five centuries later.

Incredibly, the study of Daniel has been discouraged rabbinically. Why do you suppose they have proclaimed, "Cursed is he who studies the end times"?[9] Could it be that a sincere study of the evidence leads to an unpopular conclusion? Prophecy would have no value or personal benefit without an awareness of what has been foretold and what has been fulfilled. In the case of Daniel, the facts speak for themselves. And they speak of a Messiah who came exactly when He was promised to come.

The Season of His Dwelling

But what about the birth of Messiah? We know from Micah 5:2 that He would be born in the city of Bethlehem of Judea, not in Brooklyn, New York nor in Seoul, South Korea. The documentation on Yeshua's birth and His genealogy are both solid. The details found in the first couple of chapters of both Matthew and Luke are extensive confirmations of His Messianic credentials.

How about His precise birthdate? One facet of the problem in making this kind of determination is the time-honored Hebraic custom of emphasizing the death of a person, not one's birth. This tradition carries forward today more or less in the practice of the *yahrzeit,* a commemoration of the anniversary of a Jewish person's death.

This tradition has some scriptural support, for we see an abundance of passages detailing the atoning efficacy of the death of Messiah, but none describing a redemptive consequence of His birth. The bottom line is this: we have no direct documentation of the precise birthdate of Yeshua because He lived in a Jewish culture that memorialized death instead of birth, and the authors of the Gospels wrote their books in that same environment.[10]

So where does December twenty-fifth come from? We recall that the early Church was overwhelmingly Jewish in nature. But over time, as news spread about Yeshua and more and more non-Jewish people believed in Him, the practices of other cultures began to influence the Church. One area of influence concerned this issue of emphasizing the birth of a person. Many ancient cultures practiced astrology, which teaches that the configuration of the stars and planets on the day of one's birth influences the events throughout a person's life.

While true believers in Yeshua would readily set aside the practice of astrology, the mere recognition of birthdays has survived and is widely practiced in Western culture today. We normally do not experience a tension over this custom. But it was a source of cultural conflict for the transitional Church. For that generation it became an important issue to establish the date of birth of Yeshua.

The date agreed upon was December 25, primarily as an accommodation of the Roman festival of Saturnalia, which celebrated the winter solstice. The birth of Messiah was said to be compatible with Saturnalia's themes of light returning and hope for the upcoming year. Once this step of accommodation was taken, it was easy for succeeding generations to add yule trees from Teutonic nature worship, Santa Claus and his elves, and, of course, twentieth-century shopping mall madness.

This does not mean that wholesale changes should be in order for our western culture. But at least we should be accurate in what we uphold—because there is a true blessing at the end of this quest.

A clue regarding the timing of Messiah's birth is found in the Gospel of Luke. He describes in his first chapter how the angel Gabriel appeared to a man named Zacharias while he was conducting his priestly service in the Temple. Zacharias was part of the division of Abijah, a group of priests who served one week in the month of Tammuz (mid-June) and another week in Kislev (early December). The following chart shows the chronology:

Mid-June	During Zacharias' term of service, Gabriel revealed to him that he was about to father a son when he returned home to his wife Elizabeth, who had been barren until that time (vv. 8–13).
Early to mid-July	As promised, Elizabeth became pregnant (vv. 23–24).
Late December	In the sixth month of Elizabeth's pregnancy, Gabriel appeared again, this time to her relative Miriam (known in the English as Mary). Miriam received the news from Gabriel that she was about to conceive, through the miracle of the Holy Spirit, and give birth to Messiah (vv. 26–38).
Late December to early January	Miriam conceives Yeshua.
Early January	Miriam went to visit Elizabeth, who was then nearly six months pregnant (vv. 39–45).
Early April	After a three-month visit, Miriam left for home (v. 56).

Early to mid-April Elizabeth reached full-term and gave birth to her son John (v. 57).

Late September   Nine months after conception, Miriam gave
to early October   birth to Yeshua in the town of Bethlehem (Luke 2:1–7).

Another clue involves climate and geography. According to the book of Luke, on the night of Yeshua's birth, shepherds were nearby guarding their flocks. Bethlehem is located on a high ridge between Hebron and Jerusalem. This is a cold region in mid-winter, especially at night, and at times receives snowfall. The hills during that part of the year also provide little growth for forage. Since some shepherds can be found tending their flocks near Bethlehem year round today, we cannot be too adamant on this point. But the likelihood that they would be there on December twenty-fifth is diminished. On the other hand, it was the place to be in late September or early October.

The evidence points to a specific time in the fall. It was the season of *Sukkot,* the Feast of Tabernacles. There's more. The timing is further supported by the theme of this holiday— mankind dwelling in harmony with God.

The Feast of Dwelling

During *Sukkot* the Lord commanded the people of Israel to dwell in temporary booths or tabernacles for seven days. By leaving one's home to eat and sleep outside in a *sukkah,* this practice carried an abundance of lessons to be learned. It served as a reminder of the days of pitching tents and wandering in the wilderness as well as their deliverance from bondage in Egypt. The hut stood for the trust of the people in the Lord's promise to bring them into the Promised Land. Its flimsy structure represented the temporary nature of material things in this world. And with branches for a roof, a *sukkah* enabled the light of the stars to pass through as a sign that the ultimate dwelling place of the people was to be with God.

Not only was this festival important for Israel, but it also carried great significance for all the nations of the world. As part of the Temple services of the week, seventy bulls were sacrificed. The Hebrew sages have explained that seventy was the number of nations of the world, thus the sacrifice of these seventy bulls was said to be on behalf of all nations.[11] It was a demonstration of God's all-inclusive desire to dwell with humanity.

For that very reason He sent Messiah to live among us. This is an occurrence without parallel in any religion. What greater fulfillment of God's desire to have a close relationship with mankind than for Him to actually dwell with us— *Immanuel*—and to begin that time of dwelling on the day of dwelling, the Feast of Tabernacles.

The significance of this day on the calendar goes beyond Messiah's birthday. During His years of ministry, Yeshua made a special effort to reveal God's great desire for fellowship with mankind on *Sukkot*. As the annual celebration came about, he was very much involved in its observance.

Part of the biblical ceremony of this festival was the daily pouring of water in the Temple. On the seventh day came the *Hoshana Rabbah* ("The Great Hosana"), when a priest went to the Pool of Siloam to fill a golden pitcher with water and then returned to the Temple. This water was poured into a basin before the altar in the midst of priests blowing trumpets, the singing of sacred music and the chanting of the Hallel (Psalms 113–118). This special ceremony, which came at a time of year just prior to Israel's rainy season, was a demonstration of national dependence on God for sending rain for their crops. It was in this context that Yeshua made this offer:

> If anyone is thirsty, let him come to me and drink. Whoever believes in me, as the Scripture has said, streams of living water will flow from within him.[12]

Yeshua, who sensed the spiritually parched state of the people, offered them a refreshing source of peace and hope. There is no fear of drought with Messiah. No longer do we need to look for a solution for our spiritual needs. Through Him we find overflowing satisfaction.

A second custom on *Sukkot* was the burning of bright lights. People came to the Temple with torches. Great golden menorah lampstands, with bases fifty yards high, were set up in Temple courtyard. Each menorah had four branches with large cups for oil. Young priests would climb ladders to fill the cups and to light the wicks made from the worn-out garments of the priests. It is said that the light was so bright that all of Jerusalem was lit up by them.[13]

In the courtyard below, men appeared with torches, waving them and tossing them into the air only to catch them once again. Dancers assembled, standing tiptoe and bending and leaping to the music of harp and cymbal, lyre, flute, and trumpet.[14] Long into the night the celebration continued, until the dawn of the next day.

On the day after these lights were put out, Yeshua once again revealed their spiritual symbolism:

> I am the light of the world. Whoever follows me will never walk in darkness, but will have the light of life.[15]

He made this declaration in the area of the Temple treasury, the exact same spot where, the night before, the lampstands brilliantly illuminated the darkness of Jerusalem. A fundamental quality of light is its ability to reveal the existence of things hidden in darkness. This was a fundamental role of Messiah. He would show the way to redemption, but even more importantly, he would *become* our redemption. Not only would we be able to see our failures and the obstacles before us because of His light, but we would be able to know and be known by the very source of that light.

Yeshua came and brought into focus God's commitment to dwell with His people. Perhaps the precise date of Messiah's birth is not so significant, even if the evidence pointing toward the Feast of Tabernacles is compelling. What matters most is that He did come, just as the prophets foretold.

He came as part of God's grand agenda. From Eden to Sinai to Jerusalem to wherever we may be, God is nearby, wanting our companionship and our obedience to His plan. One final stage remains in this dwelling program—eternity.

A day is coming when we who have believed in Messiah will share in that special blessing. In that day it is said:

> Now the dwelling of God is with men, and he will live with them. They will be his people, and God himself will be with them and be their God. He will wipe every tear from their eyes. There will be no more death or mourning or crying or pain, for the old order of things has passed away.[16]

God has a plan for our lives. He has already taken great steps in bridging the gap between us and Him. We must take the final step—of accepting and receiving that plan—if we desire to dwell with Him in eternity and receive the richest blessing of all.

Every year, during the contemporary synagogue observance of *Sukkot,* a traditional prayer is said. Its words are vigorous. But they are greater still when considered in the bright light of Yeshua:

A voice heralds, heralds and saith:
Turn unto me and be ye saved, today if ye hear my voice.
Behold the man who sprang forth,
Branch is his name, David himself.
Stand up! Be buried in the dust no longer!
Ye who dwell in the dust, wake up and sing.
Glad will be the people when he ruleth.
The name of the ungodly shall perish.
But to his anointed, the Messiah David, he giveth grace.
Grant salvation to the people,
To David and his seed forever,
The voice heralds and saith. Amen.[17]

CHAPTER SEVEN

THE DAY THE RABBIS BLINKED

> An error doesn't become a mistake until you refuse to correct it.
> —*Orlando Battista*

One by one they entered the Hall of Hewn Stones, the great chamber of the Sanhedrin. They were the elders of the tribes and the priesthood of Israel as well as scribes and members of privileged families from which the high priests were taken. Each of these seventy-one men was to be knowledgeable in law, the sciences, and languages.

As they had done many times before, they took their seats in the semicircle around the room. Among them were Joazar the High Priest of Israel, Annas who would soon succeed him, and Hillel the Elder, considered to be the greatest of the sages of the Second Temple period.[1] It was clear that there would be no problem in obtaining a quorum for this session. Disciples of the Sanhedrin scrambled to find a place to sit in front on the floor. Nervously they spoke in hushed tones while awaiting the convening of the meeting. For today they were about to discuss a subject that they never imagined would happen.

Then, as the *nasi,* the president of the council, stepped to his position, the room became totally silent. A moment later, the voice of the *chacham,* the "wise one," broke the silence, saying, "Councilors of Israel, on this grave and perplexing day, we are gathered to make discernment regarding the recent events in our land, namely the dethronement of the one who has ruled over us, Herod Archelaus, and the removal of our judicial authority."

The past few years had been climactic ones in the land of Judea. After the Roman conquest of the region, Herod the Great was appointed "King of the Jews" by becoming a "friend and ally" of Rome. Even though he was of Jewish descent and had lavished expenditures on refurbishing the Temple, he was the object of widespread scorn because of his allegiance to Rome, plus the building of temples to Roman deities and his brutal slaughter of the children of Bethlehem.[2]

Matters became worse upon his death when his kingdom was divided up by his three sons. One of them, Archelaus, became ethnarch, ruler of Judea and Samaria in 4 B.C.E. His reign, which lasted for ten years, was marked by moral corruption and repression. A Jewish delegation, displeased with their ruler, went to warn Caesar Augustus that something needed to be done or a full-scale revolt was about to happen.[3]

They did not anticipate what followed, however. Archelaus was banished from his position of authority and, according to the Jewish historian and Pharisee, Flavius Josephus:

> And now Archelaus's part of Judea was reduced into a province, and Coponius, one of the equestrian order among the Romans, was sent as a procurator, having the power of [life and] death put into his hands by Caesar.[4]

Archelaus was deposed. That was good. But the *shevet,* "the scepter" or "tribal staff" of Judea, was abruptly removed. That was bad. The removal of the scepter resulted in the loss of their ability to administer the Mosaic Law. Although they would be allowed to enforce excommunication and minor forms of punishment, most significantly, they would no longer be able to try capital cases. The supreme punishment of execution was the true standard of power. And now it was gone.

Josephus is not the only historian to record this ominous transaction. The Jerusalem Talmud makes this declaration:

> It is taught that more than forty years before the destruction of the Temple, capital punishment was removed from Israel.[5]

For all intents and purposes the Sanhedrin was now powerless. It was an occurrence without precedent.

The kings of Israel held their scepter continuously for centuries which symbolized their authority and permitted the administration of Mosaic Law. In the days of the divided kingdoms—Israel in the north and Judah in the south—this practice carried on. Even while in captivity in Babylon, the kingdom of Judah had its own elders, priests, and princes.[6] They had never lost their scepter and all that went with it until now.

On this day in the great chamber there was much discussion on the consequences of the actions of Rome. "How can we be obedient to *Torah* if we cannot administer justice?" asked one councilor. "We must stand against this Roman violation of our God-given rights."

"That is not the only way to look at this circumstance," exclaimed another. "To condemn to death a son of Abraham at a time when Judea is invaded on all sides, and is trembling under the march of the Roman legions, would it not be an insult to the ancient blood of the patriarchs? We must gladly set aside this practice of capital punishment."[7]

Religious practice and politics were not the only topics of concern for the Sanhedrin. Who would be the one to speak out on the delicate subject that was in the back of everyone's mind? Finally, one councilor arose and said, "My fellow elders. We are all familiar with the words of our patriarchs and prophets. What are we to do with father Jacob's prophetic blessing to the tribe of Judah where he said: 'The scepter shall not depart from Judah, nor a lawgiver from between his feet, until *Shiloh* comes; and to him shall be the obedience of the people.'"

His quotation came from Genesis 49:10. His colleagues knew quite well what the implications were. *Shiloh* means "to whom it belongs." When the scholars of Israel translated the *Torah* into Greek in the 3rd century B.C.E. for the Septuagint version of the Scriptures, they preserved this meaning by using the phrase, "the one for whom it [the scepter] is reserved." It was widely understood that the only one who ultimately qualified for this designation was Messiah. The scepter was being reserved for Messiah alone.

The rabbis had long agreed that Jacob's prophecy meant that the kingdom of Judah would retain its ability to govern itself until Messiah came. Many of them put their conclusions in writing. For example, consider the ancient targumists who translated the Scriptures from Hebrew into Aramaic, the popular dialect spoken by Jews in Babylon. When they came to Genesis 49:10, they made sure that the Messianic identity was depicted:

> Kings shall not cease from the house of Judah nor scribes who teach the Torah from his children's children until the time of the coming of the King Messiah to whom belongs the kingdom, to whom all the dominions of the earth shall become subservient.[8]

> The transmission of dominion shall not cease from the house of Judah, nor the scribe from his children's children, forever, until the Messiah comes, to whom the kingdom belongs, and whom nations will obey.[9]

"Until Messiah comes." The Sanhedrin of the early first century had a real dilemma. They knew what God's Word said. The banishment of Archelaus had taken away the scepter from Judah. The appointment of Coponius had taken away their right to rule on capital punishment in obedience to the *Torah*. These circumstances mandated that Messiah be present.

On that day of the great debate, another councilor continued the discussion by saying, "So which of you is so bold as to stand and say, 'Here am I, your Anointed One'?" He slowly turned and scanned the room. No one moved. No one spoke. He shook his head and spoke once more, "None of you. Very well, the Scripture must be wrong. Perhaps it is a scribal error."

One of the scribes in attendance quickly retorted, "You know this could not be the case. The Scripture is holy and has been preserved in its absolute purity. It is more likely that you who make interpretations have been wrong."

The debate went on. Emotions were running high. At one point, the voice of a councilor who was known for not making hasty judgments was heard. He observed, "Is it possible that the Almighty, Blessed is He, has seen fit to send Messiah at this very time, yet we are unaware of His presence?"

"My dear elder," responded the one beside him, "would we, the most learned and esteemed body in all Israel, not be the first to recognize Messiah? This most surely cannot be the case."

Confusion and panic began to set in. Finally, the president of the Sanhedrin spoke. "It is true that Messiah has not come. Who is here to testify otherwise?" The members of the Sanhedrin shifted uncomfortably in their seats. "It must be judgment. The Holy One has revoked His prophecy and His obligation."

Rabbi Rachmon gives this revealing summary of how the debate concluded:

> When the members of the Sanhedrin found themselves deprived of their right over life and death, a general consternation took possession of them; they covered their heads with ashes and their bodies with sackcloth, exclaiming, "Woe unto us, for the scepter has departed from Judah and the Messiah has not come."[10]

They had stared straight in the face of prophecy, based on the surety of God's Word, and they blinked. They should have declared as a body entrusted with the leadership over the people of Israel, "Something incredible has happened. The scepter has departed from Judah. Messiah must be here someplace. Let us all prepare our hearts to meet Him."

But this they did not do. They had lost much of their precious political power and had become blinded to God's higher calling. They did not know that a little over eleven years earlier Messiah had in fact come. Yeshua, who had been born in Bethlehem (also according to prophecy), was now being raised to their north in the city of Nazareth by his parents Joseph and Miriam. In less than a year he would come to Jerusalem and appear in the Temple.[11]

Unfortunately, an atmosphere had been created that stifled Messianic anticipation. If the leaders were not ready to receive Him, how could the rest of the people who were not as educated be expected to look for Him? A tradition was born that would have detrimental effects on the Jewish people until this very day.

Many of the scholars who shaped modern Judaism were aware about the prophecies of Daniel's seventy weeks and the scepter departing from Judah. Rabbi Rabh gives one of several similar conclusions in the Talmud:

> All of the predestined dates for redemption have passed and the matter now depends only on repentance and good deeds.[12]

Their decision to trust no longer the precision of prophecy would send shockwaves that continue to echo throughout Judaism. A philosophy would soon begin where Scripture would take on far more allegorical rather than literal meaning. Eventually, many people would view the Messiah as a figure of speech for an age of peace and harmony instead of the Prince of Peace.

Christianity would later follow this same lead by spiritualizing a great many themes of the Bible, including the nation of Israel. While the Scriptures frequently employ metaphors to communicate its message, this episode involving the Sanhedrin and the scepter of Judah demonstrates that spiritualization is a precarious undertaking.

There is a positive epilogue to this story, however. Two decades after the kingdom of Judah lost its power, Yeshua presented Himself publicly to the nation, and He was acknowledged as Messiah by a substantial number of people in Israel. Among them was a man named Joseph of Arimathea. He was "a good and upright man" and was "waiting for the kingdom of God."[13] We also know that he had become a member of the Sanhedrin.

Joseph believed that Yeshua was the Messiah. When the Sanhedrin of his time condemned Yeshua and sent him before the Roman authorities to obtain their approval for capital punishment, Joseph voted against their charges. For Joseph was not looking for power, he was looking for the kingdom of God, and he found it when he found the Messiah.

A grave mistake was made by the Sanhedrin many years ago. They missed out on the greatest blessing the world has ever known. It cannot be undone. But a favorable decision can be made by every person today who is looking for God's kingdom. The great debate continues—each of us stands in our own place of determination. We must decide for ourselves whether or not Messiah has come.

There is also some business yet to be finished. Messiah will return once again in power and majesty to claim that which rightly belongs to him—the throne of David. We share in the great hope that He *is* coming soon and, like Joseph of Arimathea, we share in the great privilege of being part of his kingdom of righteousness.

CHAPTER EIGHT

SOME OF THAT OLD-TIME JEWISH RELIGION

Then came the Feast of Dedication at Jerusalem. It was
winter, and Yeshua was in the Temple area walking in
Solomon's Colonnade. —*John 10:22–23*

It can be cold in Jerusalem in the winter. The Golden City
has seen many days when snow falls from the darkened sky
and collects on the stones beneath. The prevailing wind comes
from the west, blowing in from the Mediterranean across the
fertile coastal countryside, becoming ever cooler as it climbs
nearly three thousand feet to Jerusalem.

For those who found it necessary to be at the Temple in
winter, the eastern side of the complex provided a measure of
relief from the chilling wind. It was there in the shelter of
Solomon's Colonnade, also called Solomon's Porch, that a solitary figure was walking among the twin rows of columns. Not
far away he came upon a pile of stones that had remained
untouched for almost two hundred years. He, like many others, knew why the stones were there. He stopped and looked
at them for as long as it takes to recall a moment in history.

This day was the holiday of *Hanukkah,* a word which means
"dedication." The history of this holiday dates back to the

days between the writing of the Old and New Testaments of the Bible. Israel at that time was under the occupation of the Grecian Empire ruled by Alexander the Great. Upon his death, the empire was divided among three generals. Two of these divided kingdoms, Syria under the rule of the Seleucids and Egypt under the Ptolemies, were continually at war, and the land of Israel was caught in the middle.

By the second century B.C.E., Jerusalem and the surrounding region were under the control of the Syrians. Its leader was Antiochus Epiphanes, a tyrant who set out to eliminate every last vestige of Jewish religious life. The sacred worship structures and scrolls of the *Torah* were desecrated. The High Priest was replaced with a non-Jewish Hellenist. A Greek city was established on the Temple mount and a statue of Zeus was placed inside the Temple. The gods of the Greek pantheon were to be worshiped, including Antiochus himself. In a blatant mockery of the Biblical ordinances, a new ritual was initiated—the sacrifice of a pig on the altar.

A large number of Jewish people chose to turn away from their culture and faith and accepted this new way of life. Greek names were adopted and the traditions of Hellenism practiced. Schools began embracing Greek rationalism. With children now competing in Greek athletics, which were customarily performed naked, Jewish parents ceased circumcising their sons. Some men even went so far as to surgically reverse their own circumcisions. Israel's biblical culture was being replaced by hedonism, the doctrine that elevates pleasure as the desired goal and result of one's actions.

Though many Jews followed the decrees of the king, others refused to bow down to the Grecian gods. Many of them were martyred for their stand. Led by a priest named Mattathias and his five sons, a revolt began against the Syrians and their continual oppression. Although Mattathias died soon thereafter, one of his sons, named Judah, carried on the revolt.

Judah and his followers began calling themselves Maccabees. Some scholars believe the name comes from *makkebet,* meaning "hammer." Others say it derives from the first Hebrew letters of the words in the verse from Psalms, "Who is like Thee, O mighty LORD?"[1]

The Maccabees fasted and prayed when their battles seemed impossible. They read from the Scriptures, especially the book of Daniel, in order to find inspiration. They were convinced that the God of Abraham, Isaac, and Jacob was the sole deity of the universe and that the statue of Zeus in the Temple was a gross mockery of the Lord's sovereignty.

As the Maccabees began to have some success in their rebellion against battalions of Syrian soldiers, the Hellenized Jews were forced to make a decision. In growing numbers they joined the Maccabees and, concurrently, returned to their biblical heritage. After three years, in spite of being outnumbered, the Maccabees overcame the Syrians and regained control of Jerusalem in 165 B.C.E. It was a victory against all odds.

But when the battle was over, an imposing task awaited them in the Temple—they had to restore and rededicate it in order to resume the Temple worship. The apocryphal book of the Maccabees chronicles what followed:

> And when they consulted what to do with the altar of burnt offerings, which was profaned; they thought it best to pull it down, lest it should be a reproach to them, because the heathen had defiled it; wherefore they pulled it down, and laid the stones in the mountain of the Temple in a convenient place, until there should come a prophet to show what should be done with them.[2]

The Temple was cleansed by removing every relic of pagan worship. But not knowing what to do with the profaned altar that had once been holy, they piled up the stones outside on the Temple mount near the Colonnade. They decided to wait until a wise prophet, perhaps even Messiah Himself, would come and determine what to do with them. A new altar was erected and sacred vessels were brought into the Sanctuary once again. Then, on the twenty-fifth day of Kislev, in early winter, the daily sacrifice was resumed. The Temple had been dedicated, which meant "consecrated," or made suitable for holy service.

In later writings another tradition emerged.[3] It is said that only a small amount of holy oil could be found to rekindle the golden menorah of the Temple, only enough oil to light the lamp for one day. It would take eight days for the priests to prepare more oil that would be sanctified for use in the Temple. It would take deep faith to light the menorah, knowing that the supply was insufficient to keep the light burning. Yet that one day's supply of oil glowed in the darkness for those eight days. As a result, it was declared that a great miracle happened there.

These thoughts and more flashed through the mind of the man standing on the Temple mount as the wind whistled through the pile of altar stones. He was saddened that the nation of Israel had turned away from the biblical worship prior to the Maccabean revolt. But he took comfort in knowing that the people regained their identity and returned to the faith of their fathers. He knew that the greatest miracle that happened there was not the extended burning of the oil in the menorah, but the revival among the people.

And so, as he turned away from the rubble, and began heading back to the Colonnade, his heart yearned for another revival in his day. His passion was great for his Jewish brothers and sisters whose faith had faded once more. His desire was confirmed a few seconds later when a voice called out to him through the wind, saying, "How long will you keep us in suspense? If you are the Messiah, tell us plainly."[4]

He knew the voice well. These people who suddenly gathered around him were familiar opponents. They had watched him while he was staring at the pile of altar stones. Now they decided to test him, to see if he was bold enough to claim to be the one who could say what to do with the pile of defiled stones. Because of this popular tradition, they asked this one named Yeshua if He was the Messiah.

But He would not play their game. His concern was not what to do with a pile of stones. His burden was for their hearts of stone. He spoke directly to this issue by replying:

> I did tell you, but you do not believe. The miracles I do in my Father's name speak for me, but you do not believe because you are not my sheep. My sheep listen to my voice; I know them, and they follow me. I give them eternal life, and they shall never perish; no one can snatch them out of my hand.[5]

Did they comprehend what He was saying? No. Did they want to comprehend what He was saying? Again, no. Have you ever had a discussion with someone (or an argument!) and noticed that as you were speaking, the other person had his or her mouth half open, ready to speak at the very moment you paused? Often we do not listen to what others have to say and we jump at conclusions to find fault with one another.

This is how the opponents of Yeshua treated Him. His words bounced off their hardened souls and dissipated with the winter wind. A short time later they even picked up stones to kill Him. He stood before them and courageously answered their threat by recalling a detail from the Maccabean restoration of the Temple. He called Himself in John 10:36, "the one whom the Father set apart as his very own and sent into the world." The same word for "set apart," *hagiazo* had been used in 1 Maccabees 4:48 to describe the Temple after it had been rededicated.

The Temple was a building that was like no other structure on the face of the earth. This was the place where the glory of God was manifested. Likewise, Messiah was to be like no one else the world has ever known. He was Immanuel, God among the people, uniquely human and divine. Like the Temple that arose behind this circle of people, Yeshua was set apart from humanity. He had a calling like none other—the redemption of mankind.

As He looked upon those angry men bearing stones, the Scriptures do not say what He was thinking. But you can be sure that He was burdened for them. He may have yearned for a revival in their hearts just as the Maccabees began a revival in their era. It was apparent that it was important for the people to get back to some of that Old Time Religion—the faith of Abraham, Isaac, and Jacob.

Modern Day Maccabees

A dedication to the pure way of God should be our meditation as well. Hanukkah is called a Festival of Lights in commemoration of the rekindling of the menorah in the Temple, the pure light of God's testimony to this world. A short time later, an even brighter light followed—the Messiah, about whom it was written:

> For my eyes have seen your salvation, which you have prepared in the sight of all people, a light for revelation to the Gentiles and for glory to your people Israel.[6]

When other attractions—other lights—of this world allure us, we need to "revolt" against them like the Maccabees. We are confronted with a world that bids us to embrace its values and ways of thinking. It seduces us with alternative gods and mystical movements that promise satisfaction for our spiritual yearnings. It entices us to seek pleasure as our first and only goal and to reverse the work which God has begun in our hearts. Our world is like trees laden with much forbidden fruit.

So many people today have abandoned their faith and sought after new spiritual experiences. For the most part, it is because they have never attempted to discover the complete message of the Bible. They may never have opened its pages, but they know it is not for them. They may scoff at its teachings and say it is ludicrous to believe in the miracles and resurrection of Yeshua, but it is acceptable to believe in reincarnation and the New Age concept of becoming one with God.

We need to be true to the original biblical truths of faith in the God of Israel and His plan of redemption through the Messiah. Our lives must be dedicated to the Lord, made suitable for His holy service. But since we live in a spiritual battleground and we face many temptations to forsake this heritage, we need to muster up some courage like the Maccabees. It happened once. It can happen again.

PART THREE

REDEMPTION

CHAPTER NINE

THE POLITICALLY INCORRECT DOCTRINE

"I'm looking for a loophole."
—*The words of W.C. Fields, a lifetime agnostic, when he was on his deathbed and was found reading a Bible.*

Did you know . . .

- A cow spends 18 hours a day chewing.
- The Mona Lisa has no eyebrows.
- The highest scoring word in Scrabble is ZWIEBACK.
- Houses in Tokyo are numbered according to the order in which building permits were issued, not by location or numerical sequence.
- In 1776, many members of the new congress advocated adopting Hebrew as the official language of the U.S.

These things are all true. Many things are true, but some truth is more relevant than other truth. Some things which may be true will have no bearing on our lives. Unless you are asked to deliver a package somewhere in Tokyo, the manner in which the streets are numbered will never impact your life.

Other things will greatly impact our lives whether or not we accept them as being true. For instance, you can jump off a tall building while saying the words, "I can fly, I can fly" over and over again and actually believe it. But unless your name is Peter Pan, you can be assured that in a few moments you will face a quite literal impact.

It is truth that counts.

One of our problems as human beings is denial. When faced with some of the unpleasant facets of life, we often deny that these problems exist. A favorite means of denial is changing the meaning of words that cause us discomfort or eliminating them altogether from our vocabulary. We modify names and descriptions to suit our preferences. Today more than ever, this is evident in the term political correctness—the adaptation of language to accommodate social sensitivities.

Some terms have long been overdue in adapting their usage. Slang names for ethnic groups, while still in use, have become less prevalent. Adoptive families are now using the terms birthmother and birthfather instead of real mother or real father.

Other terms have an agenda behind them. In some circles, the poor are referred to as the economically-exploited. A recession is called a period of economic adjustment. A tax increase has become a revenue enhancement. Husband and wife has been superseded by companion or domestic partner.

The evolution of the term for people with severe physical problems has gone from the crippled to the handicapped to the disabled to the physically-challenged and now, as this book goes to press, has now reached the differently-abled.

Political correctness has spawned a number of eye-opening modifications. The city of Berkeley, California has canceled Columbus Day and renamed it Indigenous Peoples Day. Instead of using the word "fail," some educators are saying, "achieve a deficiency." The United Parcel Service uses the term "least best" in evaluating its drivers. And the renowned manhole has become the "personnel access structure."

Before long, muses Henry Beard, we can expect to call a dog who lives in the United States a "canine-American" and the Disney Channel will be showing "Snow Melanin-Impoverished and the Seven Vertically-Challenged Individuals."[1]

When it comes to the terms "sin" or "evil," it has become politically correct to use the descriptions: judgmental lapse, morally different, or ethically disoriented. Today, it's actually most politically correct not to talk about sin at all. In fact, many religions today deny that sin even exists or has consequences.

We find this philosophy most notably in New Thought religions. Christian Science, for example, teaches that:

- Sin and disease have no real existence.
- Sickness and death are a delusion of the mind.
- Evil is merely an illusion.
- We can be perfect—and we can do it on our own.

Can this be true?

One day, two men met who hadn't seen one another in a long time. The first man asked how the other man's mother was doing. The second man answered, "Not very well; she's sick." Now the first man, who happened to be a New Thought devotee, replied, "Oh, she only thinks that she is sick."

Several months later, their paths crossed again. The first man asked, "So how is your mother now?" Remembering their previous meeting, the other man answered, "Things are much worse; now she thinks she's dead."

There are some things in this world that we can deny all we want, but there is an inevitable reckoning that will affect our lives. A day of judgment is coming, and wisdom calls us to be ready for it.

Today, that is a politically incorrect message. PCspeak cries out, "Where is the tolerance when we talk about sin and judgment?" Both sin and judgment are undeniably politically incorrect, but are they real? Are the consequences true?

In the early 1600's the famed astronomer Galileo Galilei ran head-on into the institution of political correctness of his day—the Inquisition. The Church had made the position of the sun moving around the earth as official dogma. Galileo supported the theory of another astronomer, Copernicus, and used his expertise with telescopes to confirm a diametrically-opposed position—that the earth revolved around the sun. The Inquisition, with a relentless agenda and little use for hard evidence listened to Galileo's defense only briefly before condemning his stand as heretical. Galileo may not have been politically correct, but he was correct in his belief.

Galileo's point of tension was the Church in conflict with

astronomy. Our modern point of tension primarily centers around the world in conflict with the Bible. With so many people saying that truth can be found anywhere, it takes a Galilean-like stand to say: significant truth originates in the Bible. From its pages spring forth a portrayal of the attributes of God and man plus ideals for national conduct and justice and interpersonal relationships. Compared to other "holy books," why is the Bible unique?

Its principles apply to any person, in any time or place. Unlike those who deny the obvious, it makes common sense. It tells us about human nature—about our common failings. And it provides a common redemption.

Our Common Sense

Behind political correctness lies the theory of Deconstructionism, originated by the French philosophers Jacques Derrida and Michel Foucault. Deconstructionism teaches that there is no universal common reality. There are no traditional standards or previous wisdom. In their place rests individual human interpretation. What's real for you may not be real for me.

But if something is true on an elementary level, doesn't it make sense that it will not change over time? Gravity still works in the same manner today as it did yesterday. The earth has always been round, not flat. Circumstances may change, but basic laws retain their universal nature.

While the Bible is seasoned with the miraculous, it tells about basic characteristics of man and of God which are true in any age. When children honor their father and mother, and parents do not provoke their children to wrath, healthy families will tend to result. The nation that elevates righteousness will prosper. And the individual who lives in humility and with compassion for others will be highly regarded by one's peers. The common sense of the Word of God is weighty evidence for its validity.

Our Common Failings

Sometimes we are unaware that we have a problem. On July 4, 1776 in England, King George III picked up his diary at the end of the day and wrote, "Nothing of importance happened today." Little did he know in that age of slow communication that the American Revolution had begun.

He went to bed in peaceful bliss while his empire began to crumble.

Many of us go about our lives in this manner. Whether we are too busy to think about it or we discount its impact or we fervently believe in a New Age world without sin, human failure has a grave bearing on individuals and society.

Sometimes we know that we have a problem, but we do it anyway. This kind of common struggle is very much like the cars which pass in front of my house. I live on the outside edge of a cul-de-sac that has an entrance obstructed by trees. There is a large yellow sign with the words, "Not a through street" that is hard to miss. But not a day goes by without someone driving past the sign and turning onto the court in search of a certain address. Each car then reverses its direction and resumes its search on the main street.

How often we ignore warning signs in search of some lost place to visit. Many people know that drugs may be destroying their lives or that gambling is destroying their finances, but they return to the needle or the casino anyway.

Sometimes we have a problem and we realize that we need to do something about it. A great example of realization coupled with action is in the fifty-first Psalm where David confesses:

> For I know my transgressions, and my sin is always before me. Against you, you only, have I sinned and done what is evil in your sight, so that you are proved right when you speak and justified when you judge.[2]

David freely admitted his failure. The Hebrew root of the word for transgressions literally means "to break away or to rebel." Its use in the Scriptures is always in the context of people deliberately being disobedient to God and His ordinances. Along the same lines, the word "sin" carries the meaning of "missing the mark." It tells us that moral and religious standards have been set by God and that when we do not hit them on the bull's-eye, we sin. In each word we have a graphic description of our wayward actions.

Our Common Nature
But David had more to say about sin than just actions. He testifies, "Surely I was sinful at birth, sinful from the time my mother conceived me."[3]

Originally, it was accepted in the Jewish culture that people inherited a sin nature. On the day that David made the above declaration, it was a reflection of what was widely understood in ancient Israel—when Adam and Eve sinned in the Garden of Eden, the entire human race inherited a nature to commit sin. The nature serves as a root from which is born the fruit of sinful actions.

Later, in Yeshua's day, most people in Israel still held to this understanding.[4] But the climactic events of Yeshua's death and resurrection brought the issue of sin into doctrinal prominence. The followers of Yeshua remained steadfast in the original concept of sin both as action and as a nature. Those who rejected Yeshua as Messiah, however, initiated the dismantling of many key biblical doctrines which found fulfillment in Yeshua. Some rabbis began to teach that all sin could be explained solely by human actions.

Now, modern Orthodoxy claims that mankind is born completely innocent, but *yetzer hara,* the evil inclination, grows within us until a boy reaches the age of thirteen or a girl becomes twelve. At this time in life, humans become prone to temptations which were unknown to them when they were children. It is said that religious training will enable a person to overcome this evil inclination. One rabbi, Eliezer ben Yaacov, taught, "Whoever has *tephilin* on his head and arm, *tzitzit* on his garment, and a *mezuzah* on his door is assured that he will not sin."[5]

The modern Reform movement has taken this doctrinal evolution one step further and today has no tangible explanation for what leads people to do evil.

The distinction between the biblical position on original sin and the Orthodox teaching on the evil inclination may appear to be slight. Both are described as having been sown into the heart of Adam at the Fall and then transmitted to his descendants, bringing death into the world. But the rabbinical concept eliminates the need for spiritual atonement. In this way of thinking, without a fallen nature, there is nothing to redeem.

In our everyday pop theology, we would like to think of ourselves as being above sin. Adolf Hitler, Joseph Stalin, Jeffrey Dahmer, Charles Manson—those are sinners. Along with them one can include child molesters and rapists. But, you might say to yourself, don't include my grandmother; she was as harmless as a dove. Her sins and my sins aren't big enough to warrant any consequences.

Behind every sinful action lies an internal rebellion. Not every thought of hatred leads to murder, but they surely destroy relationships. Not every thought of envy leads to theft, but they consistently shape us into self-centered users of things and people. Yeshua taught that the many acts which violate civil and moral laws all originate in the heart.[6]

This was clearly the case with David. Psalm 51 was written because of a dramatic failure in his life. He was walking around on the roof of his palace when he spotted Bathsheba bathing next door. Temptation knocked, he thought about it, and he gave in. Not only did he commit adultery with her, but he arranged for the death of her husband Uriah.

Here was David—God's anointed king of His chosen people Israel—and he was violating some of God's most sacred trusts with mankind. As a result, David was considered to be a sinner like everyone else in the nation and everyone who has ever lived on planet earth.

We can agree on one very crucial point—there is something within us that leads us to rebel and to miss the mark. For sure, one way or another, we all end up as sinners. No amount of denial will make sin go away. It is real and it is critically damaging. And one sin is enough.

Our Common Consequences

We need to recognize that we were all created in the image of God, and thus we reflect His creativity and compassion. But sin is a form of pollution—it corrupts our lives, affecting them like the way a small amount of leavening affects an entire batch of bread.

Solomon understood the severity of the problem when he observed, "There is not a righteous man on earth who does what is right and never sins."[7] Adam and Eve, Solomon, you and me—we all sin, and "the soul who sins is the one who will die."[8] No exceptions.

Because of his own sin, David recognized that he faced emotional and physical consequences. And then he realized another frightening result from sin—separation from God. He pleaded, "Do not cast me from your presence or take your Holy Spirit from me."[9]

We have already touched on this dilemma in the episode of

the giving of the Law at Mount Sinai. Because of God's holiness
and our sinfulness, He will not coexist with us until the problem
of sin is removed. These are enormous consequences. Not only
have "your sins hidden His face from you"[10] here on earth, leaving you entirely without His help and blessings for as long as
you live, but the separation will continue throughout eternity.

What does that mean? It means being in a place without
the comfort of friends, without God, in utter isolation, in
complete awareness of the circumstances, and it goes on and
on and on. It has been said that hell is a Christian contriv-
ance and that there is no mention of such a place in the Old
Testament. The above description comes directly from Psalm
88, a truly foreboding chapter in the Bible. *Sheol,* the Hebrew
place of the dead, is not a blissful place of everlasting slum-
ber. It will not be the best place to spend eternity. We need a
way of escape.

Our Common Redemption
The heaviness of his sin and its consequences led David to
seek restoration from the Lord. He metaphorically asked for
cleansing and washing and then implored God to:

> Restore to me the joy of your salvation and grant me a willing
> spirit, to sustain me. Save me from bloodguilt, O God, the
> God who saves me, and my tongue will sing of your righteous-
> ness.[11]

David sought *yehsha,* meaning safety or salvation. This
word becomes in name form—Yeshua, or "The Lord Saves."
The mere fact that David makes this plea confirms his understanding of both the consequences of his sin and a way of
escape. The salvation sought by David would eventually become available to all who call upon the Lord through Yeshua,
David's own descendant.

He also used another word which carries the meaning of
salvation. He called God the one "who saves me" which comes
from the root "to be set free." Sin drags us down, makes us
captive. We cannot defeat it on our own. We must be set free.

Utopia is not the solution, for even in the Garden of Eden,
man found a way to stumble and ruin his state. It is utter
nonsense to hope that one day we will evolve into social perfection.

Birthright is not the solution, for if King David was vulnerable to the consequences of sin, how could a descendant of Israel today escape condemnation just because of bloodlines? To assume that your heritage provides an automatic free ride to eternity is a most dangerous proposition.

Neither will good deeds or religious ritual alone make a difference. In the Old Testament, an age noted for extensive rituals and requirements of righteous actions, God classified them as being inadequate without the presence of something more significant.[12] He requires sacrificial atonement, something which He Himself would provide.

As we are about to see, the perfect solution has already been given. It is both true and relevant. And it was passionately foreshadowed on Mount Moriah.

CHAPTER TEN

A PLACE IN THE BOOK OF LIFE

LAST WILL AND TESTAMENT: I owe much, I have nothing, the rest I leave to the poor.   —*Rabelais, 1553*

For three days they walked, from the land of the Philistines northeast to a place called Moriah. A father and son accompanied by two servants and a donkey—this was a common sight in those days. The boy, who was old enough to do chores and to carry on a conversation, behaved like any other child his age, running ahead occasionally to throw a rock at an imaginary enemy or dropping back to study the flora and fauna of the wilderness. With the stars at night and the clouds by day to nudge his dreams, this was the simple world of the boy named Isaac.

But for the father, Abraham, this was another story. His heart was filled with a cacophony of emotion. For oh so many years he had lived childless—considered a curse in his world—and then, just as God had guaranteed, he was given a son to carry on the incredible covenant of promise. "God really did say that He would make my offspring like the dust of the earth, didn't He?" Abraham thought to himself. "Then what is He doing telling me to take this boy up to a mountain far

away and then to sacrifice him there as a burnt offering? I'm
too old for this kind of testing."

Mostly they walked in silence as the distant mountains
drew near. Abraham continued to glance over at Isaac. His
mind could not shake off the imagery of the innocence of his
son and God's command to sacrifice him. Tears welled up in
his eyes when his emotions grew strong. Yet somehow he
pressed on with God's words echoing inside—"All the peoples
on earth will be blessed through you." With a great sigh,
Abraham's lips formed the words, "God, you know my heart. I
will be faithful to you."

Finally on the third day they came to the place set aside by
God for the test. They parted ways with the servants and the
donkey. But before they made the final climb to the top of
Moriah, Abraham left a hint of the degree of confidence in
God that remained in his heart. He turned to his servants
while placing a hand on the shoulder of Isaac and said to
them, *"We* will come back to you."

Rabbinical tradition holds that the story of Abraham and
Isaac on Mount Moriah took place on *Rosh Hashanah,* the
biblical holiday of New Year.[1] Thus the account from Genesis
22 is customarily read as part of the observance. It is a story
replete with lessons on faith and obedience. And it is also a
source of understanding of God's grand plan of redemption
for mankind.

In the previous chapter, we considered our common failings and the common consequences of our sins. But our lives
would be rather hopeless if we did not share in a common
solution for this very serious problem. It is a solution with
four parts.

God Demands a Sacrifice

Sacrifice is not well understood by most people today. It
certainly is not a feature of our western culture. We even
have a hard time giving up our material goods. The occa-
sional car that passes us by with the mocking bumper sticker,
"He who dies with the most toys wins" underscores this common attitude. Neither are we very familiar with the historical
implications of sacrifice. Since it is not part of our modern
experience, we are not likely to be interested in why sacrifice
was a widespread practice in days gone by.

As shown in the Bible, one purpose of sacrifice is worship.

Abraham understood this connection. When God demanded that he make the sacrifice on Moriah, Abraham stated that they were going up to worship.[2] Later, many diverse types of sacrifices were mandated by God for worship.

Now lest the biblical sacrificial program become branded as barbaric, we need to be reminded that animal sacrifice, in addition to being a religious ritual, was also practical. The meat was eaten for sustenance—a living creature would have to give its life in order for another to survive—a point easily overlooked in our sheltered era of packaged meat and hamburgers to go.

In the course of sacrificing an animal, the people of biblical days offered their thanksgiving to God for His provision for their needs. Sacrifice involved offering back to God a portion of what he had provided. When performed in a spirit of humility, this was a sure act of devotion. Sacrifice was also a means to convey a sense of awe concerning God's sovereignty over life and death. In this rite of worship, He was recognized as Creator and Lord of His creation.

A second purpose of sacrifice is the forgiveness of sins. Abraham was shown a clue regarding the connection between sacrifice and forgiveness when God reiterated His covenant with Abraham and his descendants: "Through your offspring all nations on earth will be blessed."[3]

What is the blessing of this covenant? Since the greatest problem that we face is our separation from God due to sinfulness, the greatest blessing that we could ever receive is to have our separation from God removed. As the Sovereign of the Universe, it is solely within God's power to deem us worthy to enter His presence. It is also His prerogative to establish the necessary means to welcome us into His kingdom. Therefore, we ought to take seriously His demands. In the Bible—the Book of the King—He stipulated His terms for forgiveness:

> For the life of a creature is in the blood, and I have given it to you to make atonement for yourselves on the altar; it is the blood that makes atonement for one's life.[4]

In order for us to be forgiven and to be welcomed into God's kingdom, there must be a blood sacrifice made on our behalf. Sacrifice was not only a cornerstone of the Mosaic Law, but preceded it and has never been rescinded.[5] God's requirement still holds—a blood sacrifice must be made for us if we are to be reconciled to Him.

God Provides the Way

Abraham faced an immense dilemma as he stood on the top of Mount Moriah. He had been told that God would fulfill His covenant through Isaac, yet now Isaac was to be slain. He loved Isaac more than anything or anyone else in the world.

Abraham began arranging the wood into an altar, stretching out the time by shifting a piece now and then. With the altar completed, he approached Isaac and gently bound his hands and feet with rope. "Look at him," Abraham thought to himself. "He trusts me with his life. I must trust in the Lord as well."

The lump in his throat returned as he hugged his son like he had done many times before. He mustered up his strength and laid Isaac on top of the wooden altar. A few seconds later his heart started pounding as he picked up the knife that lay beside him. Looking into Isaac's eyes, an entire lifetime flashed before him. He silently reaffirmed his faith in God one last time. Into the sky he raised the blade.

Suddenly the sound of a bleating ram came from a thicket nearby! God came through! A substitute was provided. The crisis was finally over.

One of the fundamental ways of learning is through observation of contrasting situations. When we can see two different ways to accomplish an objective, we can readily evaluate their effectiveness. We can determine which is better at meeting the goal.

This was the case on Mount Moriah. If Abraham was to have actually slain Isaac, his obedience to God would have remained secure. But through the substitutionary sacrifice of the ram, not only was his obedience secure, but the heir of the covenant survived. This was the better way.

Later on we see a parallel in the Levitical sacrificial system: the nation of Israel was called to observe Temple sacrifices, but it had some severe limitations. These sacrifices atoned or "covered" sins (from *kaphar,* which forms the root for *kippur,* meaning "atonement"). However, they were only adequate for the sins up to that point in time. As soon as an individual sinned again, another sacrifice was needed. And another, and another, year after year until the day a person died.

The risk of this arrangement was the necessity of one hundred percent compliance. A lifetime of faithfulness was required. This truly called for a genuine attitude of humility. But in any era, how many of us could maintain this kind of consistency? Israel, who really typified the nature of all mankind, caved in. The nation began to die spiritually. Keeping both the letter and the spirit of the Law gave way to only going through the motions without true faith and repentance.

So God foretold a better way—there would be one final sacrifice. Concerning the ultimate sacrificial Lamb, Isaiah professed:

> Surely he took up our infirmities and carried our sorrows, yet we considered him stricken by God, smitten by him and afflicted. But he was pierced for our transgressions, he was crushed for our iniquities; the punishment that brought us peace was upon him, and by his wounds we are healed.[6]

These are sobering words. In the fifty-third chapter of Isaiah, the subject—the suffering servant—is called "a lamb led to the slaughter," a "guilt offering," and "bearing the sin of many," terms with certain sacrificial overtones.

How do we know the suffering servant refers to the Messiah? Arguments can be heard today that the subject of this chapter is the nation of Israel or a nonmessianic character such as King Hezekiah.[7] The historical sufferings of the Jewish people are indeed a lamentable chronicle without parallel. Yet the application of this passage to Israel's long saga of persecution can only be traced back to Rabbi Rashi in the eleventh century.[8] Tragically, the most severe incidents of persecution have occurred after this interpretation was proposed, thus solidifying its acceptance.

However, prior to this time, the suffering servant was widely understood to be Messiah. Over one hundred years before Yeshua, the Targum of Isaiah was written. The portion on Isaiah 53 begins with these words: "Behold My servant the Messiah . . ."[9] Many more early rabbinical commentaries directly identify the suffering servant as Messiah.[10] There clearly is a discontinuity between the original and modern Jewish interpretations.

The messianic interpretation of Isaiah 53 harmonizes completely with God's plan of redemption. Just as God provided the way out of the dilemma faced by Abraham, He provided us with a way out of our spiritual dilemma. No longer would sacrifices need to be offered continually in the Levitical system. By sending Messiah, one whom was without sin, it would forever satisfy God's unyielding requirement of substitutionary sacrifice for the forgiveness of sins. This solution would last for eternity.

God Requires Our Obedience

Everything God asked of Abraham, he followed through. God said to go, Abraham went right away early the next morning. God said to take Isaac, he took Isaac. God said to offer up Isaac, he built the altar. God said to slay him, he raised the knife. Later, when God said to sacrifice the substitutionary ram, Abraham gladly carried that out when the animal appeared in the thicket. Abraham was considered faithful in the eyes of the Lord.

So what about us, what will make us faithful? Like Abraham, we need to have a sacrifice applied for ourselves. And like Abraham, we need to do it God's way. No matter how much we rationalize it, we have no other option.

On the one hand, our circumstances are much more convenient than what Abraham faced. We don't have to saddle a donkey, nor do we have to build an altar. But we do face many pressures that make it difficult to obey God. Believers in Yeshua face much ridicule in this politically correct world. We also look around us and see God's people stumble and make mistakes. In either case, it's easy to come up with excuses not to commit our lives to God.

If we are to be considered faithful and righteous like Abraham, we simply have to ask God to forgive us of our sins and to say to Him, "Thanks for providing that final, perfect sacrifice for me." It means believing in Yeshua—that God sent Him as the Messiah and the atonement for our sins.

The remnant of Israel, Jewish believers in Yeshua, made this their essential statement of faith:

> If we confess our sins, he is faithful and just and will forgive us our sins and purify us from all unrighteousness.[11]

Confession is normally thought of in terms of telling someone something that he or she does not know. But it comes from *homologeo* which literally means "same word." To confess is to line up our words with God's words. God already knows everything about us. We are only demonstrating to Him that we comprehend how we have missed the mark.

God Guarantees the Results

Confession and repentance are two inseparable themes of the High Holy Days of *Rosh Hashanah* (New Year) and *Yom Kippur* (The Day of Atonement). A rabbinical tradition holds that on these days, books are opened in heaven and our names are recorded in one of three ledgers. There is one for the righteous, one for the not-so-righteous, and one for the wicked. Almost everyone falls into the middle category but can be transferred into the Book of the Righteous (also called the Book of Life) through confession and repentance.

Thus in contemporary Judaism during the ten days between *Rosh Hashanah* and *Yom Kippur,* the people take on an attitude of repentance and pursue the healing of relationships. The person who fulfills these requirements is said to be "sealed in the Book of Life" and assured a place in the world to come.

Several years ago it was my thrill to join twelve thousand other cross-country skiers in the annual Engadin Skimarathon in Switzerland. After twenty-six miles of huffing and puffing I was able to make it across the finish line. Back home a month later, a book with the official results of the race came in the mail. Lo and behold, there on page eighty-eight was my name. Never mind the fact that 9,095 skiers finished ahead of me, my name was recorded there for posterity!

Immeasurably greater is the Book of Life. It is a biblical concept—and in this book, everyone finishes first! How important is this heavenly book? The Lord told Moses, "Whoever has sinned against me I will blot out of my book."[12] In the Day of Judgment, prophesied Daniel, "everyone whose name is found written in the book will be delivered."[13] These writings from Moses and the Prophets are confirmed in the New Testament:

> He who overcomes will, like them, be dressed in white. I will never blot out his name from the book of life, but will acknowledge his name before my Father and his angels.[14]

The practices of being repentant and healing relationships are excellent. In fact they should be part of our lives throughout the year. But as we have seen, these are not enough to secure our salvation and a place in the Book of Life. We must also have a blood sacrifice.

After 70 C.E., following the destruction of the Temple, rabbinical Judaism underwent a radical change. The sacrificial requirement was dissected from the process of redemption. A great number of people have missed the significance of this event. The common assumption today is that sacrifice is no longer needed.

Is it just random timing that the Temple was destroyed shortly after the ultimate sacrifice of Messiah occurred? In God's economy, it is the Temple and the Levitical system that is no longer needed. The requirement itself had not been annulled, but the sacrifice of the sinless Lamb of God would now last for every day to come. As the writer to the Hebrews confirmed:

> He did not enter by means of the blood of goats and calves; but he entered the Most Holy Place once for all by his own blood, having obtained eternal redemption.[15]

Every year on the Day of Atonement, the High Priest of Israel entered the Most Holy Place (also known as the Holy of Holies) to sprinkle the blood of a sacrificed goat as an offering for the sins of the people. A second animal was designated as the scapegoat and a red sash was tied around its horns. The priest then laid his hands on the head of the scapegoat and it was sent away in the wilderness, symbolic of sending away the sins of the people. It was escorted to the wilderness by a priest who waited to release the goat until a specific sign from God was given: the red sash would turn to white, signifying that God had accepted the sacrifice and forgiven the sins of the people.

This transaction was repeated annually without fail—the sash always supernaturally changed color—until one very eventful year. It was the year of the death of Yeshua. The Talmud makes this incredible concession:

> Forty years before the Holy Temple was destroyed, the lot of the *Yom Kippur* goat ceased to be supernatural; the red

cord of wool that used to change white now remained red and did not change, and the western candle in the menorah in the sanctuary refused to burn continually, while the doors of the Holy Temple would open of themselves.[16]

Some eye-opening things were taking place, among them the sign that God no longer accepted the *Yom Kippur* sacrifice. The red sash now remained red because the acceptable sacrifice had been fulfilled in the death of the suffering servant, the Messiah. And the Talmud itself confirms that this change occurred around 30 C.E.

The site where Yeshua's death took place is also not without irony. Called Golgotha or Calvary, it is on part of the same hill where Abraham led Isaac—right there on Mount Moriah. Just as Abraham was willing to give up his own son, God the Father gave His only Son so that we might live eternally. But unlike the rabbinical model of an annual cycle of writing and erasing with uncertainty, the biblical model of the Lamb's Book of Life is written permanently and assuredly.

That is the culmination of the biblical model of redemption. It is consistent and without contradiction. It has not taken a radical change of direction. It allows God to do what He does best—to work a miracle. And it allows us to demonstrate our faith in Him.

Believers in Yeshua have the rock solid assurance of sins which are forgiven and life everlasting—our very own place in the Book of Life.

CHAPTER ELEVEN

WHO'S TO BLAME?

We're all in this alone.

—Lily Tomlin

In the middle of a crowd wearing somber shades, a solitary figure stood out from the rest. In an odd juxtaposition, this small, elderly woman in black was having a problem with her camera. I walked over to where she was standing and volunteered, "I know something about cameras, would you like me to take a look at yours?" She answered, "Yes, thank you. Please do."

I had come to the former German Democratic Republic (East Germany) one year prior to the fall of the Iron Curtain as part of a delegation commemorating Kristallnacht. Exactly fifty years earlier, on November 10, 1938, the Holocaust had begun in earnest.[1] We were there to pay tribute to those who perished, to convey our compassion for the survivors, and to state publicly that we will stand against the persecution of the Jewish people whenever and wherever it should arise today.

The shutter was jammed, so I told her that the camera needed to be repaired. "What am I going to do?" she cried. "I am supposed to be writing an article along with pictures on my experience of returning to Germany for the first time in fifty years." With a little improvisation, I said, "Don't worry.

I'll take some pictures for you. They may have to come from California, but we'll take care of you."

And so we walked into the Weissensee Cemetery in East Berlin for a wreath laying ceremony. It was there as well as at a few other stops during the day that I heard her life story. It was a tale like many others. Her name was Eva. Her parents, sisters and brothers, grandparents, aunts and uncles—her entire family had perished at the hands of the Nazis. She was the sole survivor, having been rescued and taken into hiding in Norway where she had lived since that time.

Fifty years later, Eva had returned to the land of her birth. But it was now the land of death. For her and the few other survivors who were able to return for this commemoration, the experience was heavy. From time to time I would share a word of encouragement with her—a Psalm or some thoughts that I could recall from Corrie ten Boom's *The Hiding Place.* "There is no pit so deep, that He (God) is not deeper still," wrote Corrie. Those words had always held meaning for me; perhaps they would for my new friend too.

A long time passed and then, suddenly, she said to me, "Jesus was a Jew." As I nodded in agreement she quietly added, "And we Jews did not crucify him."

If ever there was a misunderstanding of epic proportions, the death of Yeshua is it. The crucifixion has become the twisted validation for much of the historical persecution of the Jewish people. And most dreadfully, many of the proponents have claimed to be Christians. This blame has led to the following conclusions:

> You [Jews] alone may suffer that which you justly suffer.
> *Justin Martyr, c. 140 C.E.*[2]

> The Jews have been disinherited from the grace of God.
> *Iraneus, Bishop of Lyon, 202 C.E.*[3]

> The Jews are a perverse people accursed by God forever.
> *Hilary, Bishop of Poitiers, 367 C.E.*[4]

> They are only fit to be butchered.
> *John Chrysostom, 387 C.E.*[5]

> . . . as wanderers ought they to remain upon the earth . . .
>
> *Pope Innocent III, 1215*[6]

> I believe that I am today acting in accordance with the will of the almighty Creator: by defending myself against the Jew I am fighting for the work of the Lord.
>
> *Adolf Hitler, 1924*[7]

The incubation of those threatening words gave birth to the brutal deeds of pogroms, ghettoes, deportations, floggings, massacres, and the Inquisition—all of which have been justified by the label, "Christ-killers." The ultimate dark moment was the Nazi Holocaust, when an entire generation was transformed into a nation with a mission—the annihilation of the Jewish people. The degree of saturation of Jewish blame for the crucifixion can be summed up in these few lines from a 1936 German children's book:

> Jesus Christ says, "The Jew is a murderer through and through." And when Christ had to die, the Lord didn't know any other people who would have tortured him to death, so he chose the Jews. That is why the Jews pride themselves on being the chosen people.[8]

Joseph Goebbels, the Nazi minister of propaganda, once claimed that if a lie were repeated often enough and long enough, it would come to be perceived as the truth. The Big Lie of the Jewish people being solely to blame for the crucifixion has certainly been repeated often and for a long time. Goebbels, unfortunately, was right.

The Big Lie is by no means a relic of the past. It is commonly espoused by neo-Nazis today. It has become increasingly a focus of the rhetoric of the Nation of Islam. One popular contemporary spokesman noted for his provocative speeches, Khalid Abdul Muhammad, has brazenly proclaimed to a packed and receptive audience:

> I'm going to go buck-wild on you . . . like a pit bull on your Jew backside. The Jews are the murderers of Jesus. If I'm lying, bring me your Torah, your scholars, your rabbis.[9]

There is no greater motivation for one's actions than to

have a theological basis as justification. This is surely the case in the historic persecution of the Jewish people. Furthermore, it has been charged that the New Testament is an anti-Semitic book. Far from it! The New Testament is filled with portions describing the love of Yeshua and His disciples for Israel. The apostle Paul went so far as to say that he would be willing to give up his own salvation for the sake of his Jewish kinsmen.[10] The New Testament has been *used,* however, by anti-Semites and others who are indifferent to the Jewish people.

A passage frequently cited by advocates of the Big Lie is in the twenty-seventh chapter of Matthew. When Yeshua was taken before the governor of Judea, Pontius Pilate, the Roman ruler asked the crowd outside what should be done with him. Their reply was to "Crucify him." And then the crowd punctuated their desire in verse 25 with the words, "Let his blood be on us and on our children."

In the eyes of some people, this text means that *all* Jewish people for *all* time are condemned and deserve punishment. Those who hate the Jewish people point to this and say, "They have cursed themselves. And God must approve, so it is our duty to carry out His condemnation."

The illusion of Jewish blame for the crucifixion has given justification for another tragic consequence—Replacement Theology. If we can say that God has condemned all Jewish people for all time, how hard is it to take the next step by saying He will no longer fulfill His covenants with them? The "reality" of this illusion is that the Church has replaced Israel in every way and that the scores of promises regarding the Messianic Kingdom must be interpreted symbolically. To its discredit, Replacement Theology applies the curses found in the Scriptures repeatedly to Israel and blessings always to the Church, even though the passage uses the name "Israel."

This is the trademark of the Adversary—inconsistency, confusion, diversion. How can we answer such justification? We must seek the clarity of the Scriptures. Regarding Matthew 27:25, three key points discredit the misuse of the verse.

First, this was a mob which did not represent all the Jewish people of that day, let alone of every generation. The context of this chapter shows that this crowd was raised up by the leaders who opposed Yeshua. In fact, on the previous day the leaders were concerned that the many followers of

Yeshua would cause an uproar if He were to be arrested publicly.[11] Their plot was carried out in darkness and their handpicked mob who provided "public sentiment" was by no means a voice for all of Israel.

Second, they had no authority to bring guilt on their descendants. Simply because an unruly mob makes brash statements, it does not mean that God is going to honor them. The individual who speaks in such a way will likely harden his own heart and will discover the personal consequences on Judgment Day. But there is no justification whatsoever to make guilt transferable. As shown in both the Torah and the Prophets, "The son will not share the guilt of the father."[12] Therefore, the mob was by no means capable of cursing later generations.

Third, the early New Testament Church carried no grudge. Peter still called those who did not receive Yeshua his "brothers."[13] He also acknowledged that those who rejected Yeshua "handed him over to be killed," but that they "acted in ignorance."[14] How does he then describe these so-called "Christ-killers?"

> And you are heirs of the prophets and of the covenant God made with your fathers. He said to Abraham, "Through your offspring all peoples on earth will be blessed."[15]

Those who hate the Jewish people call them damned and cursed. Peter calls them heirs and blessed. When confronted with the facts, we are left with this one conclusion: national and irrevocable guilt for all descendants of Israel is neither reasonable nor scriptural.

Who, then, is responsible for the death of Yeshua? Peter and John, under the inspiration of the Holy Spirit, understood the issue well. In their prayer to God, as recorded in the book of Acts, they confirmed:

> Indeed Herod and Pontius Pilate met together with the Gentiles and the people of Israel in this city to conspire against your holy servant Jesus, whom you anointed. They did what your power and will had decided beforehand should happen.[16]

Gentiles and Jews share in this guilt together. There is no easy scapegoat in this matter, like has been conjured upon

Jews or alternately upon the Romans. There is neither an absolution of responsibility for any people group. Roman soldiers and rulers, the Sanhedrin, and the belligerent mob all had visible roles in the crucifixion. But far more importantly, in the realm of the invisible—in the very souls of mankind—dwells sin, the real culprit. As we have seen, Messiah came because all humans are sinners and need permanent sacrificial atonement.

The whole world crucified Yeshua.

Moreover, it was within God's "power and will" that the death of Messiah should take place. Yeshua made this latter fact boldly apparent before He died. His words say it all:

> I lay down my life, only to take it up again. No one takes it from me, but I lay it down of my own accord. I have authority to lay it down and authority to take it up again.[17]

Rather than assigning blame, we need to see that the death of Messiah was an indispensable part of God's master plan of redemption. Though He personally suffered in immeasurable agony, His death was good for you and for me. For through His shed blood we are able to find redemption. Instead of bloating our hearts with blame, we should fill them with gratitude.

We all can share in this blessing. The Scriptures hold a special promise for the children of Israel, however. Zechariah the Prophet spoke the words of the Lord, saying:

> And I will pour out on the house of David and the inhabitants of Jerusalem a spirit of grace and supplication. They will look on me, the one they have pierced, and they will mourn for him as one mourns for an only child, and grieve bitterly for him as one grieves for a firstborn son.[18]

Perhaps it is because Israel was the nation through whom the Messiah would come. Perhaps it is because of the centuries of blame and persecution. In any event, a day is coming when the Jewish people will recognize the Messiah as the one who suffered and was pierced for our sins. It will be a day for tears, but also seasoned richly in the grace of God.

With eyes weary from recalling the horrors of the Holocaust, Eva looked at me for some sense of relief from the many burdens that she carried. She laid before me an invitation to help her sort out the confusion of alleged Jewish guilt for not only the crucifixion of Yeshua, but for the Holocaust itself.

I took a deep breath and then said, "I know what you are saying. This blame has been wrongly placed on the Jewish people for too long. It is an excuse to commit persecution used by people who really don't understand the Bible. The Scriptures say that the whole world crucified Him. It was because of the sins of the entire world that He was killed. And most importantly, it says that He willingly laid down His life; that no one could take it from Him. He did it for you and for me."

These were fresh words to Eva. She had never heard the heart of the Good News of Messiah before, only "You Jews crucified Christ." A big burden had been lifted from her shoulders. But she now had a completely new set of issues to contemplate!

Our time was short and soon we parted ways, she back to Norway and me to America (where I later sent her some pictures). But she took with her more than the experience of returning to the site of the Holocaust. She also carried the true meaning of Messiah's death.

When we are confronted with the loaded question, "Who crucified Messiah?" it is easy to point the finger and blame. It is much more humbling to look within ourselves. We need not look anywhere else. It was me—I am the one who brought about the death of Messiah.

I cannot thank Him enough.

CHAPTER TWELVE

MORE THAN JUST DESSERT

I am afraid that this cardboard-like delicacy won't go out
of fashion for a long, long time to come.
—Sholom Aleichem

Matzah is the object of much Jewish folklore. One asks the
question, "Why is it called *matzah?*" Because it is shaped like
matzah; it has holes like *matzah;* it is dry like *matzah;* and it
tastes like *matzah*. What else could it be but *matzah?*

Consisting only of flour and water, this flat bread has no
ingredient such as yeast to cause it to rise, thus giving it the
designation unleavened bread. In addition to leaving out leavening, perforations are made with a sharp-toothed wheel to
keep the dough from rising during baking.

During ancient days in the East, food could not be stored
long. So when unexpected visitors arrived, unleavened bread,
which could be prepared quickly, was baked and served.[1] In
the Middle Ages *matzah* was an inch thick, but over time it
has shrunk to the thickness of a cracker. Up until the last
century, unleavened bread was usually round. With the inven-
tion of machine-made *matzah,* the square shape became the
norm.

The special time for eating *matzah* is Passover, the Feast
of Unleavened Bread. God commanded to Israel on this holy
day, "You shall not eat anything leavened; in all your dwell-
ings you shall eat unleavened bread."[2] The children of Israel
were told to leave Egypt in haste. There would be no time to
allow their bread to rise. Therefore, in commemoration of the
Exodus, unleavened bread is a central feature of the Passover
observance and is eaten for a seven day period.

God later revealed through Moses and the prophets that
leaven typified the way sin corrupts our lives.[3] To reinforce
this message, various ceremonial worship rites involved the
use of unleavened bread.

The Evolution of Passover

The elements of the Passover service, known as the *seder,*
have evolved over time, although most changes in the past
eighteen hundred years have been in the form of additional
comments on the basic elements. We know that some portions antedate the Maccabean period (c. 165 B.C.E.) and many
more were in practice in late Second Temple times. In other
words, the manner in which Passover is kept today is very
much like the way it was kept in the day of Yeshua.

When Yeshua and his disciples gathered for their last Passover together, they would have recited the phrase, "Every
person in every generation must regard himself as having
been personally freed from Egypt." They would have chanted
the Hallel (Psalms 113–118) and said the blessings over four
cups of wine. They would have eaten the lamb, the unleavened bread and the bitter herbs. And they would have asked
three of the four questions customarily recited today by a
young boy about what makes Passover unique.[4]

Another custom, the section concerning the "Four Sons,"
was practiced in Yeshua's day. Traditionally, this portion is
used to illustrate the reason for celebrating Passover. Each
son represents a different type of person. One is wise, one is
wicked, one is simple, and one is naive and unable to ask a
question. When their questions are asked, the leader of the
ceremony is presented with an opportunity to discuss the
redemptive message of Passover.

Astonishingly, the characters represented in the Four Sons
are not just symbolic figures. In the Scriptures, we discover
that they can be found in a real life experience. A short time

before Yeshua's last Passover, He was publicly challenged by the Pharisees and the Sadducees. In Matthew 22, Yeshua was asked consecutively a deceptive question designed to entrap Him (wicked), an ignorant question about the resurrection (simple), and a common sense question about obedience to God (wise). The chapter concludes with the words, "nor did anyone dare from that day on to ask him another question" (naive and unable to ask). Wicked, simple, wise, and naive— these are the Four Sons of the modern *seder* and the "four sons" encountered by Yeshua.

Originally, the questions of the Four Sons were asked after a meal which incorporated several ceremonial rites. One rite involved the dipping of bitter herbs in salt water, symbolizing the tears shed in the bitter experience of slavery in Egypt. Another was a mysterious custom involving unleavened bread.

During the *seder,* three pieces of *matzah* are used, said to represent unity. It is commonly thought that it is a unity of the priests, Levites, and Israelites. Many people use a special cloth cover with three compartments to hold the *matzah.* The middle wafer is taken out of the pocket and is broken in two. The smaller piece is returned to the pocket, and the larger piece is wrapped in a napkin and then hidden by the leader.

The Order Is Out of Order

If you are familiar with the modern Passover order of service, you might protest, "That's not correct. The Four Sons come toward the beginning. Just take any *Haggadah* (the recorded text of Passover observance) and it will show otherwise."

That is true. The modern order places all of the questions at the beginning of the service, followed by the explanation of the Passover story and the meal. But this was not the case in ancient times.

In Yeshua's day, the meal with its mysterious rites came first, followed by the questions and the explanation of all these things. The explanation would involve retelling God's deliverance of Israel from bondage in Egypt. When the Mishnah (the codification of the Oral Law which comprises the first part of the Talmud) was completed around 200 C.E., this order was still in effect. One portion tells us:

> When unleavened bread and bitter herbs have been served,
> and a second cup of wine has been mixed, the son should put
> his questions.[5]

But in the Gemara (the two centuries of commentary on
the Mishnah which together completes the Talmud), the order has been switched. The questions have been moved up to
the beginning of the service. This form, which continues to
our present day, makes little sense because the questions
come before the the rite which would provoke the questions.
For instance, before any *matzah* is eaten, a child inquires,
"Why do we eat unleavened bread on this night?"

According to David Daube, a Jewish Oxford scholar:

> [The change] seems to have taken place about the end of
> the second or the beginning of the third century. It is one of
> the most tantalizing riddles in the history of Jewish liturgy. A
> widely accepted solution is that an orderly putting of the
> questions and an orderly giving of the reply may have proved
> difficult after a meal which included wine. . . . It is much
> more likely that the transposition was undertaken in defence
> against Jewish Christian abuses.[6]

The purpose of the Four Questions becomes clear only in
the original order. The meal was eaten including some symbolic rites, questions were asked about their meaning, and
appropriate answers were provided. But in the midst of the
explanation of the deliverance from Egyptian slavery, there
was one more mysterious rite.

The Mystery of the Afikomen

The hidden piece of unleavened bread is called the *afikomen.*
Toward the end of the *seder,* the children search for the
afikomen, and when it is discovered, they hold it for ransom.
The leader then redeems it by paying an agreed-upon price to
the children. A piece is distributed to all participants who
then eat their portion. It is a ceremony not well-understood
today and has lost its original meaning.

In the Middle Ages, people would hang a piece of the
afikomen on their houses to protect against evil. Others believed that it could be used to halt a flood or calm a stormy
sea. They, too, had lost its original meaning.

The Talmud is not much help either. In its only reference, it states:

> After the Passover lamb (or Passover meal), one may not conclude by *afikomen*.[7]

The difficulty comes in the translation of the word. Peculiarly, it is a Greek word buried in the midst of Hebrew liturgy. Some linguists believe that it is derived from *epikomoi*, meaning "dessert." Others contend that it comes from *epi komon*, which means "revelry" or "entertainment." These interpretations, widely accepted in contemporary Jewish observance, imply that there should not be anything eaten nor any party atmosphere after the meal.

Unfortunately, both of these derivations convey a shallow meaning in a celebration replete in deep symbolism. A better choice is *aphikomenos*, a verb meaning "he is coming."[8] This derivation is more closely transliterated from the Greek language. It also has direct messianic implications. Is there any further evidence to support this derivation over the others?

Since the destruction of the Temple, many rabbis have said that the *afikomen* is symbolic of the Passover lamb. Others say that the hiding ritual refers to the Messiah, the Hidden One. They reason that just as the *afikomen* is hidden away until the people are ready to eat it, Messiah is hidden until the people are ready to meet Him. Daube contends that during the Second Temple period the *afikomen* was a symbol of the expected Messiah:

> Had no ritual of the kind preserved in the Jewish Passover eve service existed, and had Jesus suddenly distributed a cake of unleavened bread and said of it, "This is my body," his disciples would have been perplexed. With such a ritual referring to "The Coming One" in existence, the self-revelation made sense.[9]

Passover is a celebration of redemption. It recalls the redemption from bondage in Egypt some 3,500 years ago and looks forward to a final redemption. The coming Messiah, represented by the *afikomen*, gave the people of ancient Israel a source of great hope. Yeshua took a tradition that was already in use and revealed its fulfillment. This occurrence is supported by the context of the original Passover order of service.

There is no question that the early Jewish believers in Yeshua included the *afikomen* in their *seders*. Some scholars say that they were the ones to originate the practice. Whether it preceded them or they began it, this is a custom intimately linked to Yeshua. Incredibly, this messianic custom has become part of the modern observance of Passover throughout Judaism. Each year, this emblem of messianic testimony is handled and eaten, but greatly misunderstood.

The messianic symbolism of the *afikomen matzah* is plentiful. It is the second of three pieces. It is baked without leavening. It has piercings. It has stripes from baking. It is broken. A price is paid to bring it back. It is hidden from the people and later revealed once again.

Messiah, the Son of God, is the second person of God's triunity.[10] He was without sin.[11] He was pierced for our transgressions.[12] By his stripes we are healed.[13] He was broken on our behalf.[14] He paid the price for our salvation.[15] And though hidden from Israel for a time, He is being received by more Jewish people today than in any time in recent history.[16] Truly this symbol is much more than dessert.

The mystery of the *afikomen* becomes an enlightening revelation when the Passover is considered in its original format. As we have seen, the meal was eaten accompanied by several symbolic rites. The curiosity arising from these acts prompted a series of questions. The response to the question of the Wise Son—"What is the meaning of Passover?"—was the *afikomen,* the coming Messiah and now the One Who Came.

The Cup of Redemption

During the *seder,* the eating of the *afikomen* is followed by the drinking of the third cup of wine. It is traditionally called the Cup of Redemption or the Cup of Blessing. Redemption refers to God's actions on behalf of Israel both physically and spiritually. The additional title of Blessing refers to the blessing of being redeemed.

This was the cup which Yeshua took and declared to represent the blood which he was about to shed, a sacrificial act that would allow our sins to be "passed over" in the Day of Judgment. As one who lived a sinless life, he was the ultimate "lamb without spot or blemish." His death, in perfect divine timing, occurred at the very moment when the paschal lambs were being slaughtered in Jerusalem.[17] Yeshua completed the work of redemption. And He is returning one day to claim His followers.

Meanwhile, the Passover continues to testify that He is the One who came and will come again.

> For whenever you eat this bread and drink this cup, you proclaim the Lord's death *until he comes.*[18]

The evidence is there for all to see. Nevertheless, an element of faith remains. When the nation of Israel set out from Egypt, they went in haste with only unleavened bread to eat and their trust in God to provide in the wilderness. There was no room for doubt. There was no one else to trust.

In our own path of spiritual redemption we, too, have a piece of *matzah* symbolic of Messiah and a trust in God to satisfy us for eternity.

The search is on for spiritual peace. Like a child searching for a hidden piece of *matzah* which he or she really doesn't understand, we are looking for meaning in our lives. The one who finds Messiah will receive abundant rewards from our Heavenly Father, the master designer of an incredible mystery that leads us back to Him.

PART FOUR

CELEBRATION

CHAPTER THIRTEEN

A TALE OF TWO TEMPLES

> The land of Israel is at the center of the world; Jerusalem is at the center of the land of Israel; the Temple is at the center of Jerusalem. —*Midrash Tanhuma, Kedoshim 10*

Late in the afternoon on a spring day, the Judean hills were becoming a patchwork blend of green and gold. In every direction there were signs of life among the rocky soil. In the Kidron valley below a man was tending to his olive trees. The sky above was changing from a perfect blue to shades of crimson. It was another magnificent day in Jerusalem.

But this one was more remarkable than at any time in recent memory. After 293 years, something dreamed impossible was about to happen—the Temple was going to be rebuilt in Jerusalem.

For nearly three centuries the Jewish people had carried the anguish of the destruction of their Holy Place. In 70 C.E. the legions of Rome under Titus had destroyed the Temple, a structure they themselves had enlarged and lavished for eighty years. It was done to put down the rebellion of Jewish zealots which had lasted for four years. Josephus provides us with this firsthand account:

> Now as soon as the army had no more people to slay or to plunder, because there remained none to be the objects of their fury, Caesar gave orders that they should now demolish the entire city and the Temple, except for the towers of Phasaelus, Hippicus and Mariamne, and part of the wall that enclosed the city on the west side [known today as the Wailing Wall]. This wall was spared. . . in order to demonstrate to posterity what kind of city it was, and how well fortified, but had been subdued by Roman valor. As for all the rest of the wall, it was so thoroughly laid even with the ground by those who dug it up to the foundation, that there was nothing left to make anyone who came there believe that it ever had been inhabited.[1]

When the Romans were finished, there was literally "no stone left upon another." These were the very words that had been uttered by Yeshua.[2] He told his disciples that one of the events that would follow his death was the complete destruction of the Temple. This was a blatant prediction in the eyes of the authorities of that day. After all, wasn't this the Temple that had been ordained by God to be erected after the conclusion of Babylonian captivity?

But as we have seen, in God's grand plan of redemption, the Levitical sacrificial system became obsolete with the sacrifice of the perfect Lamb of God, Yeshua. The failure of the red cord of the scapegoat to change color on *Yom Kippur* was a sure indication that God no longer accepted these sacrifices. The *Shekhinah,* God's manifestation of glory, was no longer present in the Temple after Yeshua's death. With these monumental changes, the building itself was no longer needed. Thus the Sovereign Lord allowed the Romans to knock it to the ground.

And so the rubble remained for nearly three hundred years. Granted, there had been plans made during the Bar Kochba rebellion to rebuild the Temple. But no steps were ever taken. However, now in May, 363 C.E., that was all about to change.

Under Constantine, Christianity had become the official religion of the Roman Empire. But when Flavius Julianus, Julian the Apostate as he became known, was crowned emperor, one of his first moves was to renounce Christianity. In order to emphasize his repudiation of the Church, he decided to "make the Temple of the Most High God rise again."[3] He would assure that Yeshua's prophecy would be thoroughly refuted.

Word spread fast. Enthusiasm for rebuilding the Temple was high. Many Jews contributed generously for the work, giving up money, jewels, and costly garments. According to Ammianus, a Roman contemporary, Julian added a large sum of Roman funds for the project.[4]

Workers came from all around. Under the direction of Julian's close friend, Alypius of Antioch, the work began with the clearing of rubble from the Temple mount area. Storehouses were erected and filled with supplies of wood and stone and precious metals. The actual building was about to begin. To mark this great event, an inscription was chiseled in a stone of the Western Wall, the lone standing portion of the Second Temple compound that had been left by Rome as a reminder of their imperial might.[5] The inscription was a quotation from the prophet Isaiah which read:

> When you see this, your heart will rejoice and you will flourish like grass.[6]

Night fell on this eve of construction. The ebony sky engulfed the scattered cooking fires and lantern lights. There was laughter in the camp of the workers. Hearts were indeed rejoicing.

Suddenly, a massive earthquake struck the region. With a mighty roar and rising clouds of dust, the hills of Judea were violently shaking. There was more. Ammianus observes:

> Frightful balls of flame kept bursting forth near the foundations of the Temple and made it impossible for the workman to approach the place, and some were even burned to death. And since the elements persistently drove them back, Julian gave up the attempt.[7]

Some people have speculated that the explosions came from gases seeping up from the Dead Sea which were released by the earthquake. Others have attributed them to direct divine intervention. What we do know is that the workers abandoned this site which was now deemed cursed. The rebuilding was no more. Julian, the mastermind of this ambitious and glamorous undertaking, unexpectedly died one month later.

Yeshua's prophecy regarding the destruction of the Temple has held true for over nineteen hundred years. But this was not the only temple prophecy that He made.

Three years before His death, a short time before Passover was celebrated, a group of people approached Yeshua in the Temple and demanded a sign from Him to prove His authority. Yeshua answered them, "Destroy this temple, and I will raise it again in three days."[8]

His interrogators naturally concluded that He was referring to the building looming behind them. They thought it was absurd that a structure which had taken forty-six years to build and still had a few refinements to be completed could be rebuilt in three days. "This man is a fool," they surely decided.

But Yeshua was talking about another temple—a figure of speech for His own body. He was talking about His coming death and His miraculous resurrection from the grave.

Resurrection was a popular topic of the day. The Pharisees believed in a future physical reunion of the bodies and souls of the dead. The Sadducees did not. The concept was certainly biblical. Daniel the prophet gave the clearest portrait of mankind's resurrection. In the same passage when he assured deliverance for everyone whose name is found written in the Book of Life, he described a coming day when:

> Multitudes who sleep in the dust of the earth will awake: some to everlasting life, others to shame and everlasting contempt.[9]

There is strong scriptural evidence for mankind's collective resurrection preceding the Day of Judgment, and there was widespread acceptance of this doctrine in Yeshua's day. But what about a second kind of resurrection—the resurrection of the Messiah?

This doctrine only makes sense as a key bridge between two distinct roles of the Messiah. The resurrection reconciles the apparent enigma of radically different portraits of God's Anointed One in the Scriptures. One Messiah who suffered and died for our sins, was resurrected, and will return to rule as King over an everlasting kingdom is a far better solution than the hypothesis that there would be two Messiahs—Messiah ben Joseph who would suffer and die, and Messiah ben David who would rule as King. It is also immeasurably better than the common practice today to throw out Messiah's suffering altogether. The resurrection of Messiah makes both of these proposals unnecessary.

David, Israel's king of renown, articulated the concept that the Messiah would overcome death. David praised God when he realized that He "would not let Your Holy One see decay."[10]

The Hebrew meaning behind the word resurrection is "vindication." It is the foremost measurement of the validity of the claims of an individual. To resurrect oneself from the dead is to vindicate everything which the person has stood for. This would be the ultimate test of the Messiah's credentials.

The resurrection of Yeshua is the very cornerstone of the faith. If He rose from the dead, we have absolute proof that God exists and that He is in control of all things, including life itself. It means that the claims of Yeshua are true and that His substitutionary death is the one means for salvation for all humanity. It also means that we have a rock-solid assurance that we will one day follow Him in our own resurrection and in dwelling with Him in the hereafter.

Paul the apostle, who was trained by the great teacher Gamaliel and became a Pharisee, grasped the importance of the resurrection. He observed:

> But Messiah has indeed been raised from the dead, the firstfruits of those who have fallen asleep. For since death came through a man, the resurrection of the dead comes also through a man. For as in Adam all die, so in Messiah all will be made alive. But each in his own turn: Messiah, the firstfruits; then, when he comes, those who belong to him. Then the end will come, when he hands over the kingdom to God the Father after he has destroyed all dominion, authority and power.[11]

But if the resurrection is false, the faith called Christianity is bogus and hundreds of millions of people are believing in a cruel lie. It would be absolutely meaningless. Yeshua would have been just another martyr. There can be no middle ground. Paul sums up this idea by stating, "If Messiah has not been raised, our preaching is useless and so is your faith."[12]

The grave of Yeshua is empty, that much is certain. Was his body taken by Roman or Jewish authorities as some people claim? When the groundswell of popular belief in Yeshua increased, these authorities could have put an end to this Messianic movement once and for all by merely displaying the body. They did not.

Was it stolen by his disciples? All of his disciples faced exile, torture, and violent death themselves in the years that followed. It is hardly likely that they would have accepted death for something they knew was a lie. People have long been known to die for causes they believe in, but not for something that they know to be false or a deception. In spite of the constant threat of martyrdom, the disciples and many others in the early Church boldly testified that Messiah had arisen from the dead.

Could Yeshua have swooned—that is appeared to die—and later resuscitated in the coolness of the tomb? This theory calls for a man to endure the trauma of crucifixion, including the piercing of his hands and feet, lashings from a cat-o-nine-tails, a crown of thorns thrust into his head, a gash from a spear in his side, survive three days without food or water in the tomb while wrapped in pungent spice-saturated grave clothes, and then push open the huge stone from the doorway of the tomb, overpower the Roman sentries, and walk away on severely wounded feet.

To believe any of these theories is to defy logic. The Holy One did not see decay. He arose by His own divine power. Death could not hold Him back. And it could not prevent Him from appearing once again to those who believed in Him.

Over the course of forty days, He appeared ten different times, to individuals, small groups, and even five hundred people at one time. The lives of these eyewitnesses were forever changed. The one named Peter, who ashamedly denied his association with Yeshua on the eve before the crucifixion, now became a man who would risk his life a short time later by preaching about the resurrection in Jerusalem, a city where it was dangerous to do so in light of recent events. It was a message that Peter would carry with him for many years until he would be crucified himself in Rome.[13]

The shocking reality of the resurrection of Yeshua forever changed the life of Peter and so many others. It galvanized their belief, giving them an unforgettable motivation to follow His teachings and to tell others about this good news. It is this same life-changing transformation that takes place today in those who believe in Him.

Ironically, the failure of Julian's Temple rebuilding project also changed the way people perceived things. Instead of refuting Yeshua's prophecy regarding the Temple, it had become all the more validated. As a result, many Jewish people at that time came to the conclusion that Yeshua really was the Messiah. In fact, within fifty years the majority of people in Palestine (formerly Judea) were Messianic believers.[14]

Other Jews came away with a deep sense of disappointment. A philosophy that earlier had begun with the failure to recognize the timing of Messiah's coming now developed into widespread doubt of the reality of the Messiah. In their eyes it seemed to be fruitless to wait for a Messiah who repeatedly did not come when they needed him the most. Not coincidentally, in the wake of these events came the finalization of the Talmud, which formed the basis for rabbinical Judaism as we know it today.

A personal Messiah began to give way to a messianic age of enlightenment. Salvation by substitutionary atonement now gave way to studying and doing *Torah*. Man's sin nature, Messiah's deity, sufferings, and resurrection—virtually everything that had been taken up in Christianity, even if it had been originally a Jewish belief—was jettisoned. This reversal of direction has tragically affected millions of Jewish people who have followed this path which was initiated in the late fourth century.

Two temples—a fiasco at the hand of Julian the Apostate and a victory over death itself by Yeshua the Messiah—have dramatically impacted our world. One has brought grief and confusion. But the other has given the world much cause for celebration.

CHAPTER FOURTEEN

WHEN IS THE CHURCH NOT THE CHURCH?

> The difference between the right word and the almost right word is the difference between lightning and the lightning bug.
> —*Mark Twain*

Every year a most peculiar phenomenon takes place in Jerusalem. Without fail, scores of people are drawn to Jerusalem who believe that they are actual biblical characters or are certain that they have the solution for world peace. In addition, some tourists with no previous psychiatric problems react to the overwhelming presence of history and religion in the city by suffering delusions. Persons with a Christian background typically believe that they are the Messiah, the Virgin Mary, or John the Baptist. Among Jews, King David and Moses are popular figures.

It is called the Jerusalem Syndrome.[1] What causes this phenomenon? Experts in Israel who deal with the problem believe that many people come to Jerusalem expecting to find a city of peace, where their troubles will fade away, but they discover a place with its own set of tensions. Unfortunately

---

for some people, this disappointment leads to a severe psychological disconnection from reality.

Long ago, a great number of persons from nations far and wide were gathering in this same city of Jerusalem. Different from those who suffer from the Jerusalem Syndrome, these individuals were drawn to the Holy City out of obedience to the Scriptures. It was fifty days after Passover. It was feast of *Shavuot,* commonly known today as Pentecost.

In chapter four we explored the tradition of the giving of the Law on the day of *Shavuot.* We discovered that Israel, as a kingdom of priests who promised to do God's will, faced the problem of separation from God caused by sin in their lives. To eliminate that problem, God sent the Messiah to serve as their mediator and to fulfill the Law.

A second tradition associated with this holiday holds another clue to God's grand design for mankind—the reading of the book of Ruth. Three reasons have been given for the tradition of reading of the book of Ruth on this day. First, the story of Ruth and Boaz takes place during harvest time, and the harvest is a focus of this feast. Second, Ruth was an ancestor of David and, according to the Talmud, David was born and died on *Shavuot.*[2] And third, Ruth became a believer in the God of Israel and, as a result, accepted the *Torah* (which we saw previously as being especially recognized on this day).

Ruth was a Gentile from the land of Moab, where the true God was not worshiped. She married a Jewish man whose family had come to Moab to escape famine in Israel. When he died, she went to Israel along with her Jewish mother-in-law, Naomi, and made this testimony:

> Where you go I will go, and where you stay I will stay. Your people will be my people and your God my God.[3]

This is a picture of God as the Redeemer of mankind—a spiritual harvest. Israel was the nation that God had entrusted with His Word, His dwelling place, and the lineage of the Messiah. But God's compassion was not limited to Israel. They were to be a "light to the Gentiles."[4] The other nations of the world were to know about the true God through their obedience and testimony. Greater still was Messiah's substitutionary death for all people in God's creation. His expression of love extends to every nation, tribe, and tongue.

We should not be surprised, then, to see the grand fulfillment of the Law and the wider extension of God's kingdom
on the very day of the feast of *Shavuot*. In chapter four we
saw how God would have to send His Holy Spirit to abide
with mankind in order to "write the Law on our hearts." That
day had come.

The second chapter of Acts tells what took place fifty days
after the ominous Passover when Yeshua was put to death.
His disciples had rejoiced in seeing their resurrected Messiah. They had witnessed His ascension into heaven. Now on
this day of Pentecost, they were gathered together in the
Temple in Jerusalem. It was at the time of day when the
Torah and Haftorah portions were read in the Temple.

> Suddenly a sound like the blowing of a violent wind came
> from heaven and filled the whole house where they were sit-
> ting. . . . All of them were filled with the Holy Spirit.[5]

In both Hebrew *(ruach)* and Greek *(pneuma)*, the word for
wind and spirit are the same. God's spirit is pictured in the
metaphor of the wind—you can't see it, but you are aware of
its presence by the changes taking place in your environment. The "wind of change" was assuredly blowing on this
day.

Jews from every direction and Gentiles who believed in the
God of Israel were present that day because it was one of the
three required pilgrimage festivals.[6] They had come from Eu-
rope, the Mediterranean, North Africa, and as far away as
modern Iran in Asia. Each one came speaking the language
of his native land. When the Holy Spirit came upon the disciples of Yeshua, they were given the miraculous ability to
speak the languages of the people who were surrounding
them.

Earlier we considered a rabbinic legend in which God took
the Law to all the nations of the world, but they refused until
He came to Israel. That same legend claims that God offered
the *Torah* to them in their native languages.[7] This theme
appears in several similar legends. It seems that God had
placed an understanding in the hearts of the sages of Israel
that He was inclined to communicate His plan of redemption
to all people in such a way that they would be able to comprehend it fully.

That is exactly what transpired on the first great day of Pentecost on Mount Sinai and on the second great day of Pentecost in Jerusalem. By miraculously speaking in the language of the diverse nations represented there, the disciples of Yeshua definitely grabbed their attention! At first it led to some confusion and even mockery (the disciples were accused of being intoxicated). But chaos soon gave way to conviction as Peter delivered an articulate message on what was taking place.

Peter, who was familiar with the tradition of David having been born and also dying on *Shavuot,* selected as part of his theme some writings of David and an illustration on the king himself. He demonstrated that unlike David whose body remained in his tomb, Yeshua had resurrected from the dead and thus provides the assurance of spiritual redemption.[8] The "special effect" of communicating in other tongues plus the proclamation of the Messianic message motivated three thousand people that day to believe that Yeshua was the Messiah of Israel.

This message was taken by these pilgrims back to their homes in distant lands. They assuredly told others about what they had witnessed and what they now believed. Soon, the disciples who had walked with Yeshua and others who joined them would begin making journeys of their own to spread the good news. They went forth accompanied and empowered by the Holy Spirit, which now dwelled within their own spirits. As promised, the Spirit would no longer come and go like gusts of wind in Old Testament days. He would now blow in a steady, powerful way, never abandoning those who welcomed Him to dwell in their hearts through belief in Messiah.

The Meaning of the Church

Pentecost is generally accepted as the day of the "Birth of the Church." At first glance, this seems clear, but we need to take a deeper look.

The spelling of the word "church" descends from the letters of the Greek word *kuriakos* meaning, "belonging to the Lord." This phrase coincides with our common understanding of the nature of the Church—people who belong to the Lord as a result of their belief in Him. But this word is only used two places in the New Testament, neither of which is a direct description of the Church.[9] The Church born on Pentecost takes its spelling from *kuriakos,* but not its meaning.

Can we actually say that the birth of those "belonging to the Lord" took place on this day? The answer is yes if they did not exist prior to that special day of Pentecost. But the answer is no if they already were present.

Back on the day when God gave the *Torah* on Mount Sinai, the people were called His "treasured possession; for the whole earth is mine."[10] They belonged to the Lord just as the entire world belonged to the Lord. Moses later continued with the image of *kuriakos* with this description: "For the Lord's portion is his people, Jacob his allotted inheritance."[11]

The faithful ones of Israel were described as "belonging to the Lord," the same word which comes into English as "church." Those who trusted in God through repentance and substitutionary atonement in the days of the Old Testament have received the same salvation as those who have repented of their sins and accepted Messiah's substitutionary atonement today. There is a continuity in God's kingdom before and after Pentecost of persons "belonging to the Lord."

Nearly 1500 years after Sinai, on that eventful day in Acts 2, the three thousand new believers gathered in Jerusalem were either Jews by birth or by conversion. And there were already faithful believers in existence—the remnant who became followers of Yeshua before Pentecost. It was not something new for people to belong to God.

So just what is different about the body of the faithful after Pentecost? The solution rests in the Greek word translated throughout the New Testament as "church" but has a literal meaning quite different than the one to which we are accustomed. It is *ekklesia,* meaning "called out ones." And indeed, this is the picture of what took place for the first time on that special Pentecost.

As individuals called out, the Church had the purpose of taking the message of Messiah to the rest of the world. When you know something to be true—as those who had witnessed the resurrection and the coming of the Holy Spirit had done—it is a strong motivation to tell others.

The logical result of the "calling out" means that people not previously part of the ones "belonging to the Lord" would become partners and share in God's blessings. Even though there were some Gentiles, like Ruth, already "belonging to

the Lord," they were few in number. This would all change
with the coming of the Holy Spirit. The day of Pentecost was
the beginning of their greater redemption.

God's all-inclusive plan was represented in a special ceremony on *Shavuot*. Two loaves of bread were customarily
waved before the Lord in the Temple on this feast day. In
contrast to the unleavened bread of Passover (symbolic of
the sinless Messiah), these were baked with leavening. They
symbolized Jew and Gentile, side by side, each one bearing
sin in their lives, equally presented before the Lord for His
acceptance.

The Scriptures say that the gathering of God's "called out
ones" would be built upon the confession that Yeshua is the
Messiah.[12] They would be called the Church.

The Church is not supposed to be a theater where you go
to be entertained and experience sensationalism. It is not
supposed to be a country club where you go for recreation and
catch up on current events. It is not supposed to be a jail
house where we face restrictions on all sides and the pastor is
the warden. Neither is it supposed to be like a gymnasium
where you get a spiritual workout nor a pub where you go to
escape from responsibility.[13] The Church is a body of redeemed
men, women, and children being equipped and deployed to
reach out in families, neighborhoods, and work places with
the good news of Messiah.

The distinction between *kuriakos* and *ekklesia* could be
called mere semantics and irrelevant to one billion people
who call themselves Christians today. However, there is an
important underlying implication that we need to keep in
mind.

Instead of just calling Pentecost the birthday of the Church,
it is more accurate to say Pentecost was the day when those
who were already "belonging to the Lord" became "called out
ones." This understanding preserves the recognition of the
legacy of the faithful ones of Israel and our calling to reach
out to others.

This, then, is the culmination of God's plan for all people—
that we would believe in His Torah and its fulfillment in
Messiah and receive the power and the blessing of His Holy
Spirit. He will knit us together in fellowship with other believers and send us forth to tell others.

God has given us much reason to celebrate.

Along with Ruth, can you say, "Your God will be my God"? To those who answer yes, we share in the promise of belonging to Him forevermore and the joy of serving Him today.

CHAPTER FIFTEEN

A MARRIAGE MADE IN HEAVEN AND ON EARTH

Since Creation, God has engaged in making matches, a task as difficult as dividing the Red Sea.
—*Rabbi Jose ben Halafta*

Marriage is a subject that is quite central to our culture. Without it we would have missed out on Ozzie and Harriet, and Archie and Edith Bunker. It has been the focus of countless books and workshops. Even the ancient rabbis found time to comment about it. Here is a sample of one of their teachings:

In their meticulous attention to detail, they noticed something hidden within the letters of the Hebrew words for man, woman and God.

> The word for man is אִישׁ *ish.*
> The word for woman is אִשָּׁה *ishah.*
> One of the names of God is יָהּ *Yah.*

Reading from right to left according to the mode of Hebrew, they observed that י *yod,* the first letter of God's name, is found in the word for man. Then they noticed that ה *heh,* the second letter of God's name, is found in the word for woman. If you take away those two letters, both words become אֵשׁ *esh,* which means "fire." The rabbis came to the conclusion that if you take God out of a marriage, all that is left is a consuming fire!

There is certainly a great deal of truth to that conclusion. But there is an even deeper message that is hidden in the biblical custom of marriage. It is the symbolism of both personal redemption and end-times events. Like many of the other traditions and customs of the Jewish culture that we have already considered, it has a powerful message for us today and it affirms the incredible message of the Bible.

As you probably might conclude, our contemporary custom of marriage has changed considerably from biblical days. Today, two people typically discover one another, fall in love, and then decide together when and how to get married (or to live together first). Parents are usually innocent bystanders as the decision is being made—that is until Mom and Dad are asked to finance the wedding and reception!

This was not the biblical method. During ancient days, marriage was a custom with three distinct phases which were very precise and structured. These phases gave marriage a solemn air of personal commitment and spiritual dedication. But they also held a tremendous underlying message.

Phase One: The Match
During the biblical era, sons and daughters alike were completely under the authority of their fathers. By law, they were permitted to marry at the age of thirteen. But in general, when most boys were sixteen to twenty years old and girls were about fifteen, they were considered ready for marriage.

Unlike their modern counterparts in the West, these young people were linked together through matchmaking. The match would be made between the heads of families—the fathers, with the father of the son taking the primary initiative. We see this custom as far back as Genesis 24 when Abraham decides that it is time for his son Isaac to wed. Sometimes a *shadchan* (matchmaker) would be used to help arrange a suitable match. In the case of Abraham it was his chief servant.

Traditionally, after matching two suitable candidates, the *mohar* would then be agreed upon. This form of dowry would be the price the young man was willing to pay for his bride. The minimum amount was said to be 50 pieces of silver. Some of the *mohar* would go to the bride-to-be and some would go to her father or the remaining family. While the father of the bride legally had authority over her, she would customarily be asked if she agreed with the arrangement. The rabbis were explicit on this point:

> A man must not betroth a daughter while she is still a minor; he must wait till she attains her majority and says, "I love this man."[1]

They understood that it was not in the best interests to force someone to marry against his or her will. Usually the fathers wanted a good marriage for their children, so the matches generally met the approval of the sons and daughters. In the story of Isaac's wedding to Rebekah, we see both the provision of the dowry gifts (v. 53) and the seeking of her consent (v. 58).

Later, a custom arose in which the father of the bride would fill two bowls or cups with wine. After they drank from the cups together, they would then be pronounced husband and wife. This ceremony was called the *erusin* or *kidushin*. In spite of its informality, this ceremony was legal and binding—it was a covenant. They were legally married at this point in time.

After the Babylonian exile, more features were added to the *erusin* ceremony. Guests would gather to add their blessing upon the couple and a feast normally followed. The groom and his parents would then return to their home and the bride would remain in her father's house until the culmination of the wedding.[2]

Phase Two: The Betrothal Period

The waiting time before the marriage culmination was an interval of about one year, or one month in the case of a widow. The bridegroom returned to his father's house where he would make preparations to receive his bride. He would build a *chadar,* a room in his father's house decorated with gold and other special provisions.

The process was not to be rushed and had to meet meticulous standards, all under the watchful eye of the father of the bridegroom. Whenever a person would ask the groom about how soon he would be going to meet his bride, he would have to defer to his father since he was the only one who could say when the time had come.

Likewise, the bride would prepare herself to meet the groom. The one-year waiting period would certify her virginity. She made clothes for the wedding party, especially for herself. She bathed in perfume and oil. She instructed her bridesmaids how to respond on the day when the groom announces his arrival. And she placed a lamp in her window, burning continually until the day he would come for her.

Phase Three: The Culmination

Finally the day came for the father to send his son for the bride. With great anticipation, the groom would leave his father's house and go to the residence of the bride.

A witness was sent to the home of the bride, where he would shout, "Behold, the bridegroom comes!" Upon hearing this announcement, the bride would come out of her home along with her attendants. A majestic procession then began. This ceremony was called the *nisuin* meaning "the carrying." She would be carried in a decorative wedding litter called an *aperion*, accompanied by her bridesmaids holding lamps of oil.

The apocryphal book of Maccabees describes what followed:

> There was much ado and great carriage; and the bridegroom came forth, and his friends and brethren, to meet them with drums, and instruments of music, and many weapons.[3]

They were treated like a king and a queen. It was the custom of the groom to wear a diadem, an ornamental cloth headband worn by kings of the East. As Isaiah informs us, the "bridegroom adorns his head like a priest."[4] The bride also wore a gold or silver headband along with an ornamental headdress and many jewels.[5]

Led by their attendants, the bride and groom would then meet and stand beneath a *chuppah*, a silken fabric canopy. In later days, the canopy was accented with gold and with purple crowning. The *chuppah* was raised at the four corners by poles carved from trees which were planted by the groom's mother and father when he was a child.

The *ketubah*, a marriage contract, was then read aloud. This document confirmed the process which began at the beginning of the betrothal. It described the obligation of the groom to honor and provide for his bride. It stipulated the *mohar*, the price the groom paid for the privilege of marrying his bride. The groom's signature represented his commitment to the agreement. The bride's signature represented her consent to the agreement. Two witnesses also would sign the *ketubah*. Blessings were then recited over a final cup of wine.[6]

At that time the procession would move on together to the home of the bridegroom. With this transfer, the bride was no longer under the authority of her father, but now under her husband. The covenant had become complete—the bride and groom would henceforth dwell together.

Their wedding would culminate with a marriage feast for invited guests marked by music and dancing and, at least in the case of Samson, telling riddles.[7] In this culture noted by festivals, the wedding celebration would last for an entire week.

Today, Jewish weddings have changed considerably. Principally, the two ceremonies have been combined into one, thus eliminating the waiting period. But some elements such as the reciting of blessings, the drinking of cups of wine, the *chuppah* and the *ketubah* have been retained.[8] More recent customs have been added and are now considered "traditional," such as the bride circling the groom in a very elegant manner.

What about the popular custom in which a glass is crushed by the groom with his foot? The favored explanation is that this is done in sorrow over the destruction of the Temple in Jerusalem. But this custom originated during the Middle Ages when the groom would throw the glass against a wall to make a loud noise in order to ward off evil spirits. For the same reason, church bells were rung after Christian weddings.[9] There is also a common joke that the smashing of the glass is the last time the groom will be able to put his foot down!

Superstition and humor aside, the contemporary Jewish wedding ceremony is still very rich in meaning and should be highly regarded. And we need not discount the essential occasion of two persons uniting in marriage. Marriage is the foundational building block of the family and society.

But there is a deeper message to be found. Within the original marriage ceremony of the Bible is a wonderful display of God's creativity and His revelation for seekers of spiritual truth.

God's Plan Revealed

Part 1: The Match	
The Biblical Marriage	*God's Plan of Redemption*
The groom is under the authority of his father.	God's Son came under the Father's authority (John 5:26–27).
The bride is under the authority of her father.	The world is under the power of the Adversary (1 John 5:19).
The father of the groom takes the initiative.	God the Father sent forth His Son to the world (Gal. 4:4).
Some people need a matchmaker.	Some people need the insights of others to understand salvation (2 Cor. 11:2).
A price is paid by the groom.	The Son paid a great price for our salvation (1 Cor. 6:20).
The bride agrees to the price.	We are saved when we accept the Son's sacrifice (Eph. 2:8–9).
A covenant is made.	The Son made a covenant with his people (Rom. 11:27).
The groom and bride drink a cup.	The Son drank the cup of death and believers share in the blessing it brings (1 Cor 10:16).
The match is made public.	Believers are to make public their faith (Matt. 10:32).

Part 2: The Betrothal Period	
The Biblical Marriage	*God's Plan of Redemption*
The groom returns to his father's house.	Messiah returned to the Father (Mark 16:19).
A waiting period begins.	We wait for Messiah's return (1 Thes. 1:10).
The groom builds a place for his bride.	The Son is preparing a heavenly place for believers (John 14:2–3).
The father decides the time to fetch the bride.	The Father decides when to send the Son again (Matt. 24:36).
The bride prepares herself for the groom.	Believers are to prepare themselves for Messiah's return (Matt. 25:1–13).

Part 3: The Culmination	
The Biblical Marriage	*God's Plan of Redemption*
A witness announces the arrival of the groom.	A trumpet and angel announce His coming (1 Thes. 4:16).
The bride comes with her attendants.	Living believers will ascend (1 Thes. 4:15).
The groom comes with escorts.	The Son brings the redeemed who have died (1 Thes. 4:14).
The groom wears a crown.	Messiah as King wears a crown (Rev. 14:14).
The bride wears a crown.	Believers receive the "crown of life" (Rev. 2:10).
They meet beneath a canopy.	We will meet beneath the heavens (1 Thes. 4:17).
The marriage contract is read aloud.	The names of believers recorded in heaven will be proclaimed (Rev. 3:5).
The bride is no longer under the authority of her father.	Believers are to be free from the authority of Satan.
A celebration begins.	A marriage feast will take place in heaven (Rev. 19:5–8).
The celebration is for invited guests only.	Only those invited by God will take part in the heavenly celebration (Rev. 19:9).
The bride and groom dwell together.	Believers will dwell with God forever (Rev. 21:3).

As Creator of the universe, our God has a real flair for innovation and artistry. There is perhaps no greater symbolic medium of His plan of redemption than in marriage. It is His most detailed and richly sculpted work. To ignore this symbol is to ignore God Himself.

But when we are keenly sensitive to His creative hand, the Bible springs to life before us. Phrases that formerly seemed like mere words are now vital links to His plan for our lives. Consider, for example, just a few of the above verses which may have once seemed peculiar or lacked deep meaning:

> In my Father's house are many rooms; if it were not so, I would have told you. I am going there to prepare a place for you. And if I go and prepare a place for you, I will come back and take you to be with me that you also may be where I am (John 14:2–3).

> No one knows about that day or hour, not even the angels in heaven, nor the Son, but only the Father (Matt. 24:36).

> For the Lord himself will come down from heaven, with a loud command, with the voice of the archangel and with the trumpet call of God, and the dead in Messiah will rise first. After that, we who are still alive and are left will be caught up together with them in the clouds to meet the Lord in the air. And so we will be with the Lord forever (1 Thes. 4:16–17).

> For the wedding of the Lamb has come, and his bride has made herself ready. Fine linen, bright and clean, was given her to wear. Then the angel said to me, "Write: 'Blessed are those who are invited to the wedding supper of the Lamb!'" (Rev. 19:6–9).

What a glorious day that will be. But in the meantime, we still have some things to do. It all boils down to readiness. God has plainly decreed that His Bridegroom, the Messiah, has been sent to marry the Bride, the Church.

Like the bride consenting to the proposed match with the bridegroom, our first and most important responsibility is to agree to the redeeming covenant put forth by God. Each one of us, in our own personal encounter with Messiah, must become matched to Him. He has declared that He will assume all the responsibility by providing us with spiritual redemption. He just needs our consent to make it a binding agreement.

After that, we are called to prepare ourselves, living lives of righteousness, in anticipation of the day of culmination. Messiah, the bridegroom, has returned to His Father's house for a period of time that the Father alone knows. But, in that coming day, the Father will send forth the Son one final time to claim His bride—His people who are willing to believe in Messiah—and desire to join Him in a banquet without end.

CHAPTER SIXTEEN

A VISIT TO THE MUSEUM

The further back you can look, the farther forward you are likely to see.
                                              —*Winston Churchill*

Wrinkled fragments of parchment covered with Paleo-Hebrew writing. Strips of leather used to bind scrolls. Linen cloths for covering the tops of terra cotta jars. Inkwells employed by scribes. Jugs, plates, cups, and pots. Each hermetically sealed display case held a different piece of treasure.

The Dead Sea Scrolls and their related artifacts had come to America for a limited tour, and it was my pleasure to spend an afternoon with them. It was intriguing to contemplate the written thoughts of people from the ancient Qumran community. It was thought-provoking to consider the implications of the controversial "Pierced Messiah" fragment.[1] So much history resting comfortably at a constant sixty-eight degrees Fahrenheit and forty-nine percent relative humidity.

Many of us view the Bible in the same way we peruse the artifacts of a museum. We read the words and try to catch a glimpse of the way people lived long ago. We can either laugh at the crude manner in which some things were done or marvel at the level of sophistication in other areas. And like walking out of the museum and getting into our car to drive home, we can discount the Bible as a book that no longer has relevance for our lives and turn to other sources for inspiration.

But the Bible is not merely an archive of the past. It is timeless in its message. God's holy inspired Word speaks to our hearts today and gives us a sure hope for tomorrow.

Time and time again, God has placed His creative trademark in the Scriptures by depicting a variety of customs that testify regarding His grand plan of redemption for mankind. He has worked behind the scenes of history to preserve that message and to provide us with clues that reveal His intentions.

At times, God has worked dramatically, like preventing the rebuilding of the Temple in the days of Julian the Apostate. But in other circumstances, His methods have been subtle, such as the many biblical customs which carry rich symbolic meaning.

You might ask the question, "Why has God gone to all this bother to be so mysterious?" Let it be said that God is very forthright in stating His will. Much of the Bible gets right to the point when it comes to God's intentions. But it is also quite clear that God is interested in people who *seek* Him. This book began with that premise recorded in Jeremiah— "you will seek me and find me when you search for me with all your heart."[2]

The true seeker of God is like a person in love with someone else. When a person says to you, "I love you," it is much more meaningful when it is a voluntary kind of love, not obligatory. God has given us enough information to let us conclude that His way fulfilled through the Messiah is the correct way. But He has still left room for faith. It is that final step of saying, "I don't understand everything, but I still believe" that makes you the kind of person in whom God is interested.

That bold step of faith is made difficult, however, by the lifelong assumptions that we carry. The traditions of men tend to obscure the traditions of God. The following folk tale illustrates that principle:

Once upon a time there was a king who had two sons. Late in his life he was struck with an illness and, sensing that he was dying, he summoned his sons. He told them, "I am not long for this world, and it is my decree that one of you will inherit my kingdom. Therefore, mount your horses and ride to the holy city of Jerusalem. The one whose horse arrives there last will be the heir to the kingdom."

The two sons left their father with hopes of great prosperity, but at the same time they were both perplexed by their father's instructions. Obediently they mounted their horses and headed off in the direction of Jerusalem. As you can imagine, neither one was in a great rush to arrive there. They took turns dropping behind each other and, as the walled city of Jerusalem appeared on the horizon, they rode slower and slower until they both came to a complete stop.

They sat in their saddles for as long as their bodies could bear, and then dismounted and sat on the ground in the shade of a nearby tree. For the rest of that day, they remained there, alternately staring at their horses and the towers of the city in the distance, all the while sitting in silence.

About the time you might think they were prepared to sit for the rest of their lives, suddenly one son bolted to his feet and jumped on his brother's horse. The other son did the same, and together they raced on toward Jerusalem, each one riding on his brother's horse. They had solved the riddle of how to assure *their own horse* would arrive last in Jerusalem and thus gain the inheritance of the kingdom.

That's the way it is for many of us on our spiritual journeys. We ride our familiar, comfortable traditions and assume that they are the only way to arrive at a philosophical destination. But by dismounting from our assumptions and spending some time seeking the true solution, whatever it may be, we will find it and then have the means to obtain the kingdom which is only a short distance away.

It doesn't matter what kind of son or daughter you might be—Jew or Gentile, rich or poor, young or old—God has a place for you in His kingdom. His solution, though perhaps hidden from you, is really quite simple. It can be summed up in three points.

First, God requires our faith:

> For it is by grace you have been saved, through faith—and this not from yourselves, it is the gift of God—not by works, so that no one can boast.[3]

Faith means that we trust God in every way, but especially regarding our spiritual redemption. It means setting aside our attempts of good works done with the hope of earning God's respect. Salvation rests solely on the shoulders of Messiah and our response to him.

Second, God requires confession and repentance from our sins:

> If we confess our sins, he is faithful and just and will forgive us our sins and purify us from all unrighteousness.[4]

Again, God is the one who changes us. He removes the consequences of sin and makes us suitable—righteous—to enter His presence. By acknowledging our transgressions and turning from them, God works the miracle of redemption.

Third, He requires our acceptance of the substitutionary sacrifice of the Messiah:

> . . . for all have sinned and fall short of the glory of God, and are justified freely by His grace through the redemption that came by Messiah Jesus. God presented him as a sacrifice of atonement, through faith in his blood. He did this to demonstrate His justice. . . .[5]

Sin causes death, but to our great benefit, Messiah became our substitute. Many people claim to believe in God and may even confess their sins to Him, but unless there is a blood sacrifice made on our behalf, the process of redemption is incomplete. We must take this last step of submission in order to be justified—to free us of condemnation and to be assured of peace with God.

Can you see the trend in God's requirements? He completes the work; we have to accept it. He is certainly much more consistent than we are! And He is more gracious as well. What a great and perfect plan He has designed for us.

We have no other option.

About Yeshua it was written:

> Salvation is found in no one else, for there is no other name under heaven given to men by which we must be saved.[6]

Those are strong words. But as we have seen, it is a statement supported historically and is consistent with God's plan and His attributes. But He leaves it as an open invitation before us. And the truly astonishing thing about it is—it's free! Our salvation comes at no cost to us—Messiah paid the price for all.

If you have already believed in Yeshua and received his gift of spiritual redemption, the words of this book ought to be an encouragement to you and an affirmation that your belief is absolutely rock solid. What you have already taken by faith is backed up by prophecy, history, and a series of mysterious customs which simply cannot be explained by coincidence. Your challenge is to continue digging and seeking and growing in maturity.

But if you have never taken that step of faith, make that your commitment today. Leo Tolstoi once astutely observed, "Everyone thinks of changing the world, but no one thinks of changing himself." Salvation is a very personal thing. We have to decide for ourselves. God has laid out His terms and now patiently awaits each and every one of us to come to Him and receive His free gift.

One final question remains. What about the customs themselves? If they held meaning in biblical days, they can still be meaningful today. For the Jewish believer in Yeshua, the traditions of one's heritage need not be forsaken. Likewise, the Gentile believer can broaden his or her worship experience through celebration of the biblical holidays. It's the best of both worlds.

The kingdom of God stands before us, with its gate open wide and with plenty of room for everyone inside. From the entrance stretches a path that passes your way and has been walked by countless others before you. Together we have the joy and the privilege of citizenship in the kingdom and taking part in the only truly everlasting tradition.

CHAPTER NOTES

Chapter 1

1. For a detailed analysis of contemporary trends, see Leith Anderson, *Dying for a Change* (Minneapolis: Bethany House Publishers, 1990).
2. 1 Kings 19:18.
3. One century earlier, King David commissioned a census in which 800,000 men who were old enough to fight in combat were counted (2 Sam. 24:9).
4. Rabbi Gamaliel, (Acts 5:39).
5. Eusebius, *History Book IV* 5:1–2. See also Louis Goldberg, *Our Jewish Friends* (Chicago: Moody Press, 1977), 28.
6. C.E., the "Common Era" and B.C.E., "Before the Common Era" are the academic equivalents to B.C., "Before Christ" and A.D., "Anno Domini."
7. Abraham Rabinovich, "The Judeo-Christians in Israel," *The Jerusalem Post* (December 11, 1993, p. 9).
8. Stefano Assemani, *Acta Sanctorum Martyrum Orientalium et Occidentalium,* Vol. 1 (Rome, 1748), p. 105.
9. Babylonian Talmud, Sukkah 49*b*.
10. Jeremiah 29:13 (NASB).

Chapter 2

1. Genesis 1:27.
2. Genesis 32:30.
3. Isaiah 63:8–16.
4. John 15:13.
5. Luke 10:25–37.
6. Psalm 27:11.
7. Proverbs 9:9.
8. In contemporary practice the *mezuzah* is touched and fingers are then kissed when entering and leaving a home.
9. John 14:2–3.
10. Since the dye for the blue thread came from a Mediterranean snail that is unknown in our modern era, the practice of including a blue thread has been discontinued.

Chapter 3

1. The procedure for observing *Shavuot* is described in Leviticus 23:15–22.
2. The origin of these customs are not completely known, but according to some sources, these restrictions are kept in memory of the 24,000 disciples of Rabbi Akiva who fought in Bar Kochba's army. It is said that "all of them died between Passover and Pentecost."
3. Psalm 73:2–5, 16.
4. Psalm 73:17, 28.
5. Micah 6:6–8.
6. Isaiah 1:11–20.
7. These words are based on 1 Corinthians 13.

Chapter 4

1. As indicated in Exodus 12:6 and Leviticus 23:5, Passover began on the evening of the fourteenth day of the first month *(Nisan). Shavuot,* the Feast of Weeks or Pentecost, was to occur fifty days after the Sabbath (Lev. 23:16), which would be at the beginning of the month of *Sivan.* The giving of the Law is prefaced in Exodus 19:1 with the words, "In the third month *(Sivan)* after the Israelites left Egypt, on the very day, they came to the Desert of Sinai." Accounting for the three days of preparation, it was

determined that the Law was given on *Shavuot* (see Pesahim 68*b*).
2. Exodus Rabbah 27:9.
3. Exodus 19:16–19.
4. Isaiah 59:2.
5. Galatians 3:24.
6. Ezekiel 36:26.
7. Ezekiel 36:27.
8. Joel 2:28, 32.

Chapter 5

1. Berachot 35*a*.
2. Superstitions abound concerning the role of the supernatural in sneezing. The custom of wishing good health can be found in Roman, Greek, German, and Scandinavian cultures. The phrase, "God bless you" probably originated during the plague of 590 when excessive sneezing preceded death. This practice was viewed later in light of many folk religions. It is said by some that when invoking this blessing, witches or fairies could not work evil on the sneezer. Others believed that a demon was attempting to pronounce your name and could thus capture your soul unless the blessing was said.
3. Genesis 12:3.
4. Matthew 1:1–16.
5. Numbers 16.
6. 1 Corinthians 12.
7. Deuteronomy 33:26.
8. Mark 10:16.
9. Ephraim and Manasseh are represented because they were especially beloved by Jacob and because, as shown in Deuteronomy 33, Joseph's tribe received a double portion of blessings.
10. Mark 10:15.
11. The modern Jewish practice is never to kneel, except as part of the observance of Yom Kippur. The prohibition against kneeling is not biblical in origin but rabbinical as a reaction to the common practice in some branches of Christianity.
12. Mark 10:21.

Chapter 6

1. Exodus 25:8.
2. Isaiah 7:14.
3. Isaiah 9:6.
4. In Isaiah 7:14 the Hebrew word used is *almah,* which literally meant a "young maiden of marriageable age." Although the root meaning is not physical virginity, as expressed in the word *betullah,* it carries this connotation. Unlike our modern culture, in biblical days a maiden was a virgin. To be unchaste would have brought shame on her family and would have severely defiled the marriage process (see chapter 15). With this understanding the ancient rabbis used the Greek word for physical virginity, *parthenos,* in the Septuagint translation (Second Century B.C.E.).
5. Daniel 9:25.
6. Ezra 7:11–26; Nehemiah 2:1–9.
7. For a thorough description of the timing of this prophecy, see *Chronological Aspects of the Life of Christ* by Harold Hoehner (Grand Rapids: Zondervan, 1977), pp. 115–139, or an earlier work by Robert Anderson, *The Coming Prince: The Seventy Weeks of Daniel with an Answer to the Higher Criticism* (Grand Rapids: Kregel Publications, 1984).
8. Zechariah 9:9; Matthew 21:1–11.
9. Rabbi Samuel ben Nahmani declared in the name of Rabbi Jonathan: "Blasted be the bones of those who calculate the End, for they used to say, 'Since the (time of the) End has arrived, but he has not come, he will never come'" (Sanhedrin 97*b*). Rabbi Jose ben Halafta said, "He who declares the End has no share in the world to come" (Derekh Eres Rabba 11).
10. Even Luke, the sole Gentile author of the New Testament, received his factual information from eyewitnesses who were all Jews.
11. Babylonian Talmud, Sukkah 55*b*.
12. John 7:37–38.
13. Mishnah Sukkah 51*a*.
14. Tosephta Sukkah 4.
15. John 8:12.
16. Revelation 21:3–4.
17. From the *Hoshana Rabbah* service, as found in most congregational prayer books.

Chapter 7

1. Josephus, *The Complete Works of Josephus*, trans. William Whiston (Grand Rapids: Kregel Publications, 1981), *Antiquities* XVIII 1:1; 2:1; Babylonian Talmud, Shabbat 15*a*; Sifrei Deuteronomy 357.
2. Matthew 2.
3. Josephus, *Antiquities* XVII 13:2.
4. Josephus, *Wars of the Jews* II 8:1.
5. Jerusalem Talmud, Sanhedrin 18*a*; 24*b*.
6. Ezra 1:5–8.
7. John Lightfoot, *Horae Hebraicae: Evangelium Matthaei* (London, 1658), 275–276; Babylonian Talmud, Avoda Zarah 8.
8. Targum Yerushalmi Gen. 49:10 (Jerusalem Targum).
9. Targum Onkelos Gen. 49:10 (The official targum used in the synagogue service).
10. M. M. Lemann, *Jesus Before the Sanhedrin,* trans. Julius Magath (Nashville: Methodist Episcopal South Publishing House, 1886), 30, 38; Ramon Marti, *Pugio Fidei* (1651), folio 251; and Babylonian Talmud, Sanhedrin Chap. 4, Folio 37, recto. See also Fred Meldau, *Messiah in Both Testaments* (Denver: Victory Publishing Co., 1956), 30.
11. Luke 2:41–52.
12. Babylonian Talmud, Sanhedrin 97*b*.
13. Luke 23:50–51.

Chapter 8

1. Psalm 89:8 (NASB).
2. 1 Maccabees 4:44–46.
3. The earliest versions of the Hanukkah story are found in the First and Second Books of Maccabees. But with the exception of a brief mention of relighting the Temple lamps, there is nothing said regarding a miracle. In this source, the observance is instituted for eight days because *Sukkot,* the eight day Feast of Tabernacles, could not be kept that year. Only in the Gemara (the later rabbinic material), Shabbat 21*b*, do we find the first reference to a miracle in an event which took place over four hundred years earlier.

4. John 10:24.
5. John 10:25–28.
6. Luke 2:30–32.

Chapter 9

1. Henry Beard, *The Official Politically Correct Dictionary and Handbook* (New York: Villard Books, 1993).
2. Psalm 51:3–4.
3. Psalm 51:5.
4. Samuel S. Cohon, *Essays in Jewish Theology* (Cincinnati: Hebrew Union College Press, 1987), 240.
5. Bavli Menahot 43*b*. See also chapter 2 of this book.
6. Matthew 5:21–28; 15:19.
7. Ecclesiastes 7:20.
8. Ezekiel 18:20.
9. Psalm 51:11.
10. Isaiah 59:2.
11. Psalm 51:12, 14.
12. Isaiah 64:6; 1:11–14.

Chapter 10

1. Tanchuma, Vayero 22:13.
2. Genesis 22:5.
3. Genesis 22:18.
4. Leviticus 17:11.
5. The sacrifices offered by Abel (Gen. 4:4) and Noah (Gen. 8:20–21) were favorably accepted by God. Jacob makes a similar sacrifice in Genesis 46:1.
6. Isaiah 53:4–5.
7. Sanhedrin 98*a*, 99*b*.
8. Solomon ben Isaac (Rashi), *Commentary to Talmud*.
9. Targum Pseudo-Jonathan, Isaiah 52:13.
10. Sanhedrin 93*b*, 98*b*.
11. 1 John 1:9.
12. Exodus 32:33.
13. Daniel 12:1.
14. Revelation 3:5.
15. Hebrews 9:12.
16. Babylonian Talmud, Yoma 39*b*.

Chapter 11

1. On the night of November 9–10, 1938 violence broke out in Germany and Austria against Jewish communities. Nazi sympathizers vandalized hundreds of synagogues, burning 191 houses of worship. 7,500 Jewish-owned shops were looted, nearly 30,000 Jews were arrested, and 100 others were murdered. Kristallnacht, as it has come to be known, was a major turning point in the Nazi "Final Solution."
2. Justin Martyr, *Dialogue with Trypho,* 16.
3. Iraneus, *Against Heresies,* 3:21.
4. Paul Grosser and Edwin Halperin, *The Causes and Effects of Anti-Semitism: The Dimensions of a Prejudice* (New York: Philosophical Library, 1978), 78.
5. John Chrysostom, *Discourses,* I 3:2.
6. Malcolm Hay, *The Roots of Christian Anti-Semitism* (New York: Liberty Press, 1981), 81.
7. Adolf Hitler, *Mein Kampf* (Boston: Houghton Miflin, 1939), 64.
8. Elvira Bauer, *Don't Trust the Fox in the Green Meadow Nor the Jew on His Oath,* 1936.
9. Khalid Abdul Muhammad, speech given at the University of Wisconsin-Milwaukee, March 25, 1994.
10. Romans 9:3. Paul was not the first to make such an extreme statement. When confronted with the failings of the people of Israel, Moses replied to God, "But now, please forgive their sin, but if not, then blot me out of the book You have written" (Ex. 32:32).
11. Matthew 26:5.
12. Deuteronomy 24:16; Ezekiel 18:20.
13. Acts 2:29.
14. Acts 3:13, 17.
15. Acts 3:25.
16. Acts 4:27–28.
17. John 10:17–18.
18. Zechariah 12:10.

Chapter 12

1. See Genesis 18:6.
2. Exodus 12:20 (NASB).
3. Leviticus 6:17; Hosea 7:4.

4. Three of the four questions were already in use while the Second Temple was standing. The inquiry regarding the bitter herbs came later.
5. Pesahim 10.
6. David Daube, *The New Testament and Rabbinic Judaism* (London: Athlone Press, 1956), 193–194.
7. Pesahim 119*b*.
8. *Aphikneomai*, the root form of the word becomes *aphiknomenos*, "the coming one" as a perfect passive participle and *aphikomen*, "I came" in the aorist (past) tense. See Liddel-Scott, *A Greek-English Lexicon* (Oxford: Clarendon Press, 1968), 290, and *The Analytical Greek Lexicon* (London: Samuel Baagster and Sons, 1895), 62.
9. Daube, *He That Cometh* (London, 1966), 10.
10. 1 John 5:20.
11. Hebrews 4:15.
12. Isaiah 53:5.
13. Ibid.
14. Matthew 26:26.
15. 1 Corinthians 6:20.
16. Romans 11:23–24.
17. Matthew 27:45; Mishnah Pesahim 58*a*.
18. 1 Corinthians 11:26.

Chapter 13

1. Josephus, *Wars of the Jews* VII 1:1.
2. Matthew 24:2 (NASB).
3. Flavius Julianus, *To the Community of the Jews,* 369a–398a.
4. Marcellinus Ammianus XXIII 1:2.
5. The Western Wall, also known as the Wailing Wall, was a retaining wall at the base of the Temple mount and was not part of the Temple proper.
6. Isaiah 66:14.
7. Ammianus, XXVIII 1:3.
8. John 2:19.
9. Daniel 12:2.
10. Psalm 16:10.
11. 1 Corinthians 15:20–24.
12. 1 Corinthians 15:14.

13. Origen says that at his request, Peter was crucified upside down in deference to his Messiah.
14. Jacob Neusner, *Judaism in the Matrix of Christianity* (Philadelphia: Fortress Press, 1986), 20–21.

Chapter 14

1. Clyde Haberman, "What Makes Samson Run Amok? He's Manic in Jerusalem," *New York Times* (May 13, 1992), A13.
2. Mishnah Rosh Hashanah 25*a*.
3. Ruth 1:16.
4. Isaiah 49:6 (AV).
5. Acts 2:2, 4.
6. The other feasts in which Israelites were required to go up to Jerusalem were Passover and Tabernacles.
7. Midrash Tanhuma 26*c*.
8. Acts 2:24–38.
9. *Kuriakos* is used in 1 Corinthians 11:20 where it refers to the "supper belonging to the Lord" and in Revelation 1:10 where it describes the "day belonging to the Lord."
10. Exodus 19:5.
11. Deuteronomy 32:9.
12. Matthew 16:16.
13. My thanks to B. Wayne Hopkins for the inspiration for this analogy.

Chapter 15

1. Babylonian Talmud, Kiddushin 13*a*.
2. Madeleine S. and J. Lane Miller, *Harper's Encyclopedia of Bible Life* (New York: Harper and Row Publishers, 1978), 101.
3. 1 Maccabees 9:39.
4. Isaiah 61:10.
5. For a description of the glamorous state of the bride and groom, see Psalm 45.
6. Alfred Edersheim, *Sketches of Jewish Social Life in the Days of Christ* (Grand Rapids, Mich.: Eerdmans Publishing Co., 1972), 149.
7. Judges 14:10–18.
8. In the modern *ketubah,* especially in the reform movement,

there is no mention of the dowry and it often includes mutual responsibilities. Some people put in writing the actual vows of the ceremony.

9. Alfred Kolatch, *The Jewish Book of Why* (Middle Village, New York: Jonathan David Publishers, 1981), 42.

Chapter 16

1. Fragment 4Q285, as it is formally known, measures 1.5 inches by 2 inches. It was withheld from public access for forty years by the scholars who tightly controlled the Scrolls. In 1991 an upheaval within the realm of the researchers led to the release of many of these suppressed artifacts. 4Q285 is the first nonbiblical text to contain a reference to an individual like Isaiah's suffering servant. While not all scholars agree, one of its lines can be translated, ". . . and they will put to death the leader of the community, the Branch of David." For a more detailed view of these fragments, see Robert Eisenman and Michael Wise, *The Dead Sea Scrolls Uncovered* (Rockport, Mass.: Element, Inc., 1992).
2. Jeremiah 29:13 (NASB).
3. Ephesians 2:8–9.
4. 1 John 1:9.
5. Romans 3:23–25.
6. Acts 4:12.